W9-BSL-292

For Bea—

With Joy & Love!

Barbara Joiner

Count it all Joy

"God, You Did Good!"
Other Stories
and Prayer Poems

Barbara Joiner

WMU, SBC
Birmingham, Alabama

Credits:
Cover design by Barbara Ball; photographed by Joseph Veras
Back cover photos by Clay Allison

Quotations taken from:
Life 101 by John-Roger and Peter McWilliams. Copyright 1990 Prelude
Press. All rights reserved. Used by permission. *Yes Is a World* by James
W. Angell. Copyright 1974 Word, Incorporated. All rights reserved.
Used by permission. *To Kiss the Joy* by Robert A. Raines. Copyright
1973 by Robert A. Raines, published by Word, Incorporated. All rights
reserved. Used by permission. *encounter!*, July-September 1982.
Copyright 1982 The Sunday School Board of the Southern Baptist
Convention. All rights reserved. Used by permission.

WMU, SBC
Birmingham, Alabama

©1991 WMU, SBC
All rights reserved.

ISBN: 1-56309-018-X
W913108•0394•2.5M4

Dewey Decimal Classification: 248.4
Subject Headings: CHRISTIAN LIFE
                  MISSIONS
                  DEVOTIONAL LITERATURE

To Homer--
My friend, my encourager, my beloved. He is chief among all the joys I count.

Joyful thanks to:

The Lord—whose finger writ again! Thank goodness!

Gina Howard, my editor, and *Ella Robinson,* her assistant—who made me believe I could write this book, who encouraged me and laughed and cried with me.

Rosie Bedsole, Stuart Calvert, Pat Sullivan, Bernadotte Phares, Margaret Burks, and all the other wonderful friends—who prayed me through.

Harry Atchison, Billy Reed, Sis Wallace, and *Sonya Lefkovits*—friends who filled in the gaps.

Murrel Mullins and *Nancy Rasco*—who listened endlessly to the written pages.

Dana Vansant and *Terry Ward,* my sons-in-law—maybe they will believe my wild stories now that they are in print! But then again . . .

Jackie Vansant and *Jennifer Ward,* my beautiful daughters—who have shared their mother endlessly and still love me!

Megan and *Dane Vansant,* my precious grandchildren—who are glad the book is finished so I can play!

Contents

Count It All Joy

In 1990, I finally agreed to write down some of the experiences I have been talking about for years. I did this grudgingly with full expectations of a long, dreary winter ahead. However, as I began the arduous task, my thoughts and pen raced. For the first time in my so-called writing career, I relished having pen in hand or typewriter before me. I was reluctant to go out to speak. I actually refused invitations to go out to eat! Remembering has been a great joy!

My friend, Alabama's WMU executive director, Beverly Sutton, has warned me that nobody will ask me to speak again since they can read it all in this book. I find that promising. I'll simply say, "I'm so sorry that I can't come. Just read Chapter 10."

From the first I wanted to title the book *Count It All Joy*. I realize that passage from James 1:2 says more than those four words. It says, "My brethren, count it all joy when ye fall into divers temptations." This verse is entirely appropriate for me; I am prone to fall into sticky situations as well as divers temptations! One of my biggest problems is that nearly always, sooner or later, I find the situations hilarious. And nearly always, sooner or later, God pulls me out of the miry clay. Thank goodness!

Joy has always been my touchstone. I claim joy verses as my own:

"The joy of the Lord is your strength" (Neh. 8:10).

"Thou wilt shew me the path of life: in thy presence is the fullness of joy" (Psalm 16:11).

"These things have I spoken unto you, that my joy might remain in you, and that your joy might be full" (John 15:11).

"Your joy no man taketh from you" (John 16:22).

"Rejoice with joy unspeakable" (1 Peter 1:8).

THIS I BELIEVE.

One of my favorite books, tattered by many readings, is Robert Raines' *To Kiss the Joy*. In the chapter entitled "Kiss the Joy as It Flies," I found my philosophy for living. Raines says, "The significance of his life is not to be measured in terms of its length, but in terms of the depth of his every day, the fullness, the totality, the wild, open abandon with which he gave himself, day by day, to his days."

Raines also quotes the poem "Eternity" by William Blake:

"But he who kisses the joy as it flies
Lives in eternity's sunrise."

"To kiss the joy as it flies," Raines says, "is to live in the Spirit; it is to live boldly, immediately, with gracious abandon, daring to risk much, willing to give oneself. It is to live for a moment in unison with our dream; to see the sun shining in the eyes of the smallest creatures; to create the marvelous by contagion."

YES, THIS I BELIEVE!

In his wonderful book, *Yes Is a World*, James W. Angell says, "Joy, it has been suggested, is the happiness we feel when we have faced adversity and survived." Angell also reminds us "Life isn't necessarily fair. It doesn't have to be, to be filled with glimmerings of the beautiful and worthy. What matters more than anything else is the human spirit and its determination to 'hang in there' regardless of circumstance."

OH, YES, I BELIEVE!

I've just discovered the book *Life 101* by John-Roger and Peter McWilliams. They say, "Joy seems to be something that can take place no matter what else is going on, no matter what other thoughts are being thought, no matter what other feelings or physical sensations are being felt."

I BELIEVE THIS, TOO.

Join me for a few stories and a few prayer poems. Experience the joy, the joy without which my world could not stand, that same joy with which, like Paul, I would finish my course.

—Barbara Joiner
March 1991

2

*I had a heavy accent by age two; when my mother
called for me, I answered in my best Hungarian,
"Vat do you vant?"*

Somebody Should Have Told Me
I Had a Miserable Childhood

I was born at the tail end of the depression in March 1932.
However, the depression did not end for our family until World
War II. I know this because my daddy, George Martin Horn, told
me. As a child, I didn't have the faintest notion of our extreme
poverty. I had a perfectly wonderful childhood.

I was born in Lineville, Alabama, but when I was 14-months-
old, our family moved to Columbiana into a big two-story house
with one bathroom and three other families. I thought it was
fantastic. From birth I have loved people.

Our next-door neighbors were Max and Dottie Lefkovits. Mr.
Max had come to America from Hungary in 1886 with a back-
pack of goods to sell. His backpack grew into The Columbiana
Leader, to my mind, the finest department store in the world.

I loved Mr. Max and would sit in his lap, listening to his stories for hours. I had a heavy accent by age two; when my
mother called for me, I answered in my best Hungarian, "Vat do
you vant?"

I adored Miss Dottie. She fed me bagels, cream cheese, lox,
and other exotic bits. The rest of my family may have been hungry during those lean days, but Miss Dottie kept me well. I hate
to admit it, but I had become an accomplished con artist by age
three. I convinced Miss Dottie that my mama, Lela McCrary
Horn, did not keep a kosher kitchen. Of course, we had no
meat and very few dairy products in our home. We had lots of
beans and cornbread, and that's about as kosher as you can get.
To keep me kosher, Miss Dottie fed me most of my meals.

The Lefkovits were practicing Jews, regular attenders of the
Synagogue in Bessemer, 50 miles from Columbiana. Years later I

3

discovered that Mr. Max was also a charter member of the Men's Bible Class of the Columbiana Baptist Church. Maybe that's why it was so easy for them to celebrate Christmas with me my first December in Columbiana. Miss Dottie ordered a doll from the catalog. I promptly named her "Sears and Roebuck." She was my first toy and the most beloved of my childhood.

Two other strong influences directed my preschool days: the Baptist church and the county library.

The church was about two blocks from our house. I don't remember anybody taking me to church; I think I just wandered in. I loved everything about it, but Sunbeams was my favorite. Thomas Thurman, Southern Baptist missionary to Bangladesh, asked me several years ago what made my heart beat missions. I told him the only thing I could think of was that I learned to sing "Jesus Loves the Little Children of the World" before I learned "Jesus Loves Me."

During these formative years, I happened upon revivals. In those days revivals were two, sometimes three, week happenings. Sometimes there were tent revivals. I can still smell the sawdust, but the singing captivated me. I learned to sing alto before I entered first grade. I could read the words before that.

It was common practice to reward small children to memorize Scripture verses during revivals. Miss Dolly Jones, a Presbyterian woman who attended the Baptist church, was my benefactor. She would pay me 50 cents for a short verse and a whole dollar for a long verse. I always went for the long verses. I had to recite the verse in front of the revival crowd. Miss Dolly said I put "a lot of feeling" in my reciting. A ham was born.

My favorite Sunday School teacher was Mrs. Johnnie Wood. She had a practice of making a birthday cake for each student. She baked the first birthday cake I ever had. Mrs. Wood also became my first Girls' Auxiliary (GA) leader. And I loved GAs even more than Sunbeams. No one had to push me to become involved in Forward Steps; Forward Steps turned me on.

I was stymied on the first step, however. The Maiden step required each girl to learn a series of Scripture verses that explained how to become a Christian. The first verse was Isaiah 53:6: "All we like sheep have gone astray; we have turned every one to his own way; and the Lord hath laid on him the iniquity of us all." That verse made absolutely no sense to me. I had never been very sheep-like. I was only nine, so I hadn't had many opportunities to go astray.

I went to my brother for an explanation. Ross Mullins, my older half-brother, was respected and admired by everybody who knew him. He explained Isaiah 53:6 to me. One of the things he said was that I was already a pretty rotten kid at nine (did he know about my con artist activities?). He also pointed out that I wouldn't get any better. He explained to me that God loved me anyway; that if I had been the only little girl in the whole world, God still would have sent His Son to die on the cross for me. No one had ever explained it to me in such simple words. I was deeply touched. I could hardly wait until Sunday morning. I wanted the whole world to know that I wanted Jesus to be my Saviour.

The third great influence on my life was the county library. The first housing of the Shelby county library was in the beautiful white marble county courthouse. It was three blocks from our house, so it took me a little longer to discover. Books were a real luxury in those days. We had none at our house, but the library had hundreds.

I became an avid reader. In fact, when I entered first grade, I ran away the first day. My mother was horrified. I explained to her that Miss Gertrude Bishop, my teacher, read "baby" stories. I had read all of them years before. Obviously, I concluded, I was above schooling. My mother deemed otherwise. Back I went. The only thing that kept me pacified were the library books I snuck into the classroom to read while the rest of the class plodded along with Dick, Jane, and Spot.

Reading opened up a whole new world to me. I discovered the "Twin" series right off. These were books about twins from many different countries of the world. I don't remember the name of the author, but I remember there were dozens of the books. I read every word of every book and I vowed to visit every country I read about.

An added bonus during my preschool years was a new baby sister, Nancy. She was sick frequently and took up a lot of my mother's time. I suppose that was the reason I could explore and visit and read to my heart's content. I loved Nancy to distraction. I even saved her life. Nancy managed to open the car door while we were driving to town. She fell out. I jumped out behind her and caught her on the first bounce! She was virtually undamaged. She owes it all to me that she is the beauty of the family! Another sister, Judy, was born when I was nine. She is the brain of the family. They still refer to me as "the other one."

Someone should have told me I had a miserable childhood. I never suspected it for a moment. No wonder I count it all joy. I've been surrounded by wonderful people all of my life.

Little girl with dirty face,
With half a sash dangling in space,
I see the wonder in your eyes,
I see your sites set in the skies.
What made you long to see the earth,
What made you dream from day of birth?

Thank you, Lord, for making children so
That all they do down here below,
Is gossamer wings and sparkling snows,
Wrapped in songs and tied with bows,
Packed to the brim, carried by love,
Covered with blessings from the Father above.

I want to be like that again, Lord . . .

I can?

*"It is a prime location," he said.
"It is a dump," said I. I have never had the gift of
exhortation.*

Moving On Up

The summer before I entered first grade, the Horn family fortunes took a turn for the better. Daddy opened an electrical and plumbing shop in the one room still standing of the historic Leonard Hotel across from the courthouse.

"It is a prime location," he said.

"It is a dump," said I. I have never had the gift of exhortation.

We also became proud owners of our first home, a small five room house on Sterrett Street. It was just a block-and-a-half up the hill from our old house on Main Street. We were so proud of that dilapidated old house. It was heated by a huge wood-burning stove in the kitchen. The bathroom was out the back door and down the path between the barn and the pig pen. I imagined myself on an African safari each trip I made.

A whole new neighborhood was mine to explore. The first day I discovered my guardian angel. (She still is today.) Margaret Stinson lived one house over from us. She was beautiful and brilliant; I followed her around like a devoted puppy. She spent hours trying to improve me. She washed and fixed my hair. She tried to make a high soprano out of me. She'd say, "Barbara, standing on your tip toes does not make you sing higher." She tried desperately to make a lady out of me, but it was hopeless. I've had strong tom-boy genes all of my life.

The "hill" was populated with fascinating people. Margaret's mother, Annie Kate Stinson, was one of my favorites. Annie Kate loved movies. Columbiana had a picture show where the features changed often, three times a week plus a Saturday "shoot-em-up" and a yearlong serial. When I first moved to Sterrett Street, the admission was ten cents. Children under 12 went free.

Annie Kate and I walked to the movies every time the feature changed. That was living! Even after children had to pay a dime and adults a quarter, Annie Kate bankrolled me in order to have a walking buddy. I became an avid movie fan and a devoted Annie Kate fan.

Annie Kate also taught me to embroider. However, she was not accomplished with the needle herself and I learned to sew just like her. I still have a pitiful sampler that we designed and I sewed at age nine.

Another precious neighbor was Uncle Doc Bearden. Uncle Doc was retired, but he had been Columbiana's first police-man/night watchman. An unlikely law man, Uncle Doc was short, fat, and jolly, but his stories made him sound tougher than Wyatt Earp. I spent many hours on the Bearden's front porch listening to stories and playing checkers. I can still hear that old swing squeaking.

Uncle Doc also supplied the Horn family with water. He had a well house in the back. It was actually a pavilion, roofed and lined with benches on three sides. Blue morning glories climbed to the top. The floor was cool concrete. The water drawn from the well was ice cold on the hottest August day.

A tiny room stood behind the well house. Uncle Doc's sister, Emma Farr, lived there. Tiny, stooped, and quite old to my childish eyes, I was convinced that she was a witch. Mama would send me over with a bowl of soup or such and I'd go after uttering many prayers for protection. Miss Emma always pulled out a treasure for me to admire—a colorful bowl, a tattered Spanish shawl, a flower she had picked. One day she asked me to open the bottom drawer of her dresser. I did; an enormous snake was coiled in the drawer!

"I never have any rats with Sadie living here," she cackled. That settled it—she was definitely a witch!

After Miss Emma died, Miss Lena Cox moved into the little house. She moved from the much larger Cox family home and brought everything in it to the little house. Because she had so little room, she visited around in the neighborhood as much as I did! She was a delightful, inventive storyteller and I loved her. When I got married, Miss Lena gave me two treasures: a lead crystal pitcher that had belonged to her mother, and her old Purefoy Cookbook, copyrighted first edition 1937. (The Purefoy Hotel was a Talladega, Alabama, landmark since 1920. People came from everywhere to eat at the Purefoy. Menus were featured in the front of the cookbook. The one entitled Our Regular Everyday Dinner featured six meats and a dozen vegetables along with many side dishes.)

On the other side of our Sterrett Street home was the lovely old Lester house. Homer and Elizabeth Lester Bearden lived there, along with other family members. By far the most impressive member of the family was their live-in man of all work, Mose Sutton. Mose, an enormous black man, lived in a little building behind their well house.

It was Mose who taught Dan Harper, a nephew of the Beardens, and me to shoot marbles, throw a baseball, and shoot an air rifle. We admired him tremendously. One of the saddest days of my childhood concerned my friend, Mose. He came running to our backyard. Mama was coming out of the garden.

"What are you doing with that bloody knife, Mose?" she asked.

"Oh, Lordy, Mrs. Horn, I just killed somebody," he cried.

It was a bad day on Sterrett Street when they put Mose in the slammer. However, when the investigation was complete, Mose was freed. He and Dad Robinson had been gambling and Mose won. Dad pulled a knife and a fight began. All the witnesses swore that Dad fell on the knife, that Mose acted in self defense.

Mose stayed a brief time in Columbiana after that—long enough to save the town. The Standard Oil plant had a terrible fire. The cry went out to evacuate the town. "It's going to blow," the police chief declared, "and blow Columbiana right off the map!" Fire departments from all over the county and from Birmingham fought the blaze. Mose said, "I can turn off the main valve. Give me two raincoats and keep the water hoses on me." Mose walked through fire and saved the town. I was not surprised.

The best of the folks on the hill, however, were my parents, George and Lela Horn. They were pretty colorful themselves.

Shortly after Daddy was born in Clairmont Springs, Alabama, (a popular resort during his childhood) his mother, Emma Jenkins Horn died. His daddy, Larry Madison Horn, remarried soon. But George went to live with Windman and Dora Jackson, his sister and her husband, in nearby Lineville.

His life was never easy. As a young man, he followed his older brother, Paul, to Florida to work for the Florida Power Company. He was very proud that he helped string the lines through the swamps for a budding new city—Miami.

Paul was killed working on hot wires. Daddy was knocked from the high pole in the same accident. The doctors said he'd never walked again. He went back to Lineville to recuperate, and to walk again. I get my stubbornness from him.

He met my mother, Lela McCrary Mullins, when he came back to Lineville. They were married and opened a restaurant to try to eke out a living in those hard depression days. Daddy did the cooking. He was an awful cook. They would not have made it in prosperous times!

Mama had been born outside Lineville, and had married Grady Mullins when she was only 14. Two years later, she had a little boy, Ross. The marriage was a sad one. By the time Ross was seven, Lela and Grady divorced. Mama worked in my Uncle Jessie's store in Lineville trying to support herself and her little boy. I always think of my mother when I read 2 Corinthians 4:8,9: "We are pressed on every side by troubles, but not crushed and broken. We are perplexed because we don't know why things happen as they do, but we don't give up and quit. We are hunted down, but God never abandons us. We get knocked down, but we get up again and keep going" (The Living Bible).[1]

Mama was the finest woman I've ever known. She worked hard and sacrificed for her family; her faith sustained her.

Mama loved Christmas in particular. All her Christmas gifts were ragged by Christmas morning. She shook and prodded each one in hopes of determining its contents. The Christmas of 1954, four months after my wedding, was the first that I could afford more than a token gift for her. She had wanted a nice lace tablecloth for years. I found the prettiest one in Birmingham and I wrapped it with much care. It was very heavy and had to be able to withstand Mama's fierce examinations.

She had a cerebral hemorrhage on Christmas Eve, and never regained consciousness. Faith kept me serene and strong during her 11-day hospital stay. However, when we returned to Sterrett Street after her death, that unopened gift lay beneath the shedding Christmas tree. The flood gates opened; I wept for all the unopened gifts that would never be; I wept for all the lost love and laughter. It was over too soon, but I count the precious time I had with my mother all joy.

---

[1] *The Living Bible*, copyright 1971 by Tyndale House Publishers, Wheaton, Illinois. Used by permission.

Lord,
I thought the color of pain would be red.
That's the way I feel—
Raw, bleeding, stripped with agony.
But, it's not red—it's gray.
My mind is gray; I see gray.
I feel like the bleakest, coldest winter day.
Tears aren't coming on the outside.
But inside I'm flooding with gray tears
tinged with vilest green,
swamp black,
crawling brown.

Then, I see light!
Why, it's You, Lord—right here in the midst of
gray.
You put your arms around me and love me.
Go away, gray.

I had read about Adoniram and Ann Judson and I was awed to be in such a holy place. I knew they had never touched foot there, but it was named for them and that made it hallowed ground!

I Would Not Have You Ignorant

After being sent back to school on that first day in first grade, I decided to make the best of it. After all, Paul said, "For I have learned, in whatsoever state I am, therewith to be content" (Phil. 4:11 KJV). My mother quoted this verse a lot.

Geography did it. In my mind, I climbed the Himalayas, yodeled from the Alps, and steered my houseboat all over Hong Kong harbor. The Twins books had started me down the world-awareness road. Geography just kept me roaming the globe.

Great teachers kindled my imagination and encouraged me to excellence. I did not always perform as they expected, but I nearly always gave it my best shot.

Shortly after I entered Shelby County High School, my life changed dramatically. Daddy remodeled the house on Sterrett Street. (Business was booming.) He ended up tearing it to the ground and building a four bedroom, two bathroom house. To our family, it was a mansion! In addition to indoor plumbing, we also had both an electric stove and refrigerator—and a phone! This was to be my home until 1988 when my husband and I built our dream house on Mount Dixie two miles out of Columbiana.

The second big change was I decided as a seventh grader that I wanted to be a doctor—preferably in deepest, darkest Africa. I started college prep that year. I also had a conference with Dr. James Howard Crawford, Columbiana's only physician. He immediately hired me to assist him. I made a 50 cent piece every Saturday for the rest of my high school days. By the time I graduated, I was cleaning wounds, sewing up, and cutting sutures. It was fascinating work, and I gladly worked as many as ten hours each Saturday. That's a nickel an hour and probably more than I was worth!

The third major change was triggered by my attendance at Queen's Court at Judson College. This was the gala activity for GAs who had passed the level of Queen in Forward Steps. When I reached the Queen Regent step, the wife of the associational missionary, Mrs. B. B. Curry, decided that I should be in a coronation service. She talked the WMU at First Baptist, Columbiana, into paying $5 and my daddy into paying the other $5 to send me to Queens' Court. Mrs. Curry and a friend came from Wilton to drive me to Calera to catch the bus. She bought my ticket to Marion.

It was my first real adventure. By myself I rode to Marion, changing the buses twice. I walked from the bus station to Judson College. I had read about Adoniram and Ann Judson and I was awed to be in such a holy place. I knew they had never touched foot there, but it was named for them and that made it hallowed ground!

My awe turned to dismay when I learned that I could not be in the coronation. I didn't have a crown, or a scepter, or a cape. Doris DeVault, youth secretary in Alabama, hugged me and said, "I have all three of those, Barbara. I'd love for you to have them." God has always sent the most wonderful people to supply my needs!

Queens' Court contributed more than royalty to my life. For the first time, I heard and met "real live" missionaries. I heard challenges to put Christ first, to make Him Lord of all. I knew that I had not done that. I had accepted His saving power but not His leadership each day and in each phase of my life. I made that commitment at Judson.

How He changed my life! He gave me a hunger for His Word. I always did my daily Bible reading, but it was mechanical, forced. I asked Him to help me understand and appreciate. I'll always believe that He sent the new exciting translations just for me! My prayer life changed. I started to listen more and talk less. I started my first prayer list. Praying as I went about my daily routine became a habit and a joy.

God surprised me about studying. I had done enough to make *A*'s and a few *B*'s. But He showed me that mediocrity was not what He desired; He wanted my best. I hit the books harder.

Top-notch teachers guided me: Miss Mary Peters, Miss Aileen Pope, and Mrs. Myrtle Johnson. But two were very instrumental in my life: Ellen Ruth Isbell and Marianna Davis.

Ellen Ruth Isbell, "Teacher," was not only my teacher but also my friend and confidante. I skipped a grade in school, taking summer classes, just to be in her homeroom. When she married I was one of her bridesmaids; she was one of my bridesmaids when I married.

"Teacher" was beautiful inside and out. She was a faithful worker in the Baptist church and an example of what a Christian should be. She is still my heroine and I love her very much.

Marianna Davis taught English and directed the school plays. When I was an eighth grader, she decided that I should enter the *Birmingham News-Age-Herald* oratorical contest. The subject was Racial and Religious Tolerance as a Means to Lasting Peace. I wrote an impassioned speech and I refused to change a single word. How hard we worked on that contest. Often I rode home with Marianna after school to keep on working. She lived in a big, spooky house, her old family home. I expected to see Emma Farr around every corner!

Finally, I was ready. We made it through county, then district, and all the way to state. Marianna talked Daddy into two new dresses. I felt like a fashion plate! We went to Birmingham for the contest, were guests at the Redmont Hotel, were regally entertained. The contest was held at Birmingham-Southern College. When I was announced as the junior high school winner, I was on top of the world!

Many activities occupied my time in high school. Two were favorites. I loved cheerleading. It was my kind of thing; I'd be cheering when we were six touchdowns behind. I never gave up! My other favorite was boys. I *did* like boys. Mama would not let me date until I was 15. She would allow me to go with a group to the movies or to parties. Oh, there were lots of ways to get around no dating.

One of the first real dates I had was with Homer Joiner. His cousin, Betty Bentley, was having a birthday party/wiener roast at the fire tower out beyond Joinertown. He had Betty ask me if I would go with him.

"I thought he was going steady with that "June-girl" that he's been going with since the third grade," I said to her.

"She moved," Betty replied.

I guess there would never have been a "Homer and Barbara" if "June-girl" had not moved to Georgia!

We went to the party and kept on going all through high school. We didn't go steady; I didn't believe in that. However, there was one brief, golden time when I had a Friday night boyfriend, a Saturday night boyfriend, and a Sunday night boyfriend. I loved it. After a time, Friday said, "I am all or nothing at all." That was the end of Friday. I just knew he'd miss me and want that night back. He just promptly got a full-time girl.

I decided I liked Saturday (Homer) best and should say good-bye to Sunday. On the day I'd decided to break up, he came early in the morning to see me. He explained that his dad was wanted for transporting stolen cars across state lines.

"You should break up with me so that you won't be tainted by all this mess," he said. (I still remember that old-fashioned word: *tainted*.)

"No way," I declared. "You need a friend now."

Sunday and I remained good friends all through Shelby County High, through his four years at Georgia Tech, even until he was killed on an engineering assignment when his plane crashed in the jungles of Brazil.

I not only liked boys, I liked great boys.

Some people recall their school days with misery. Not I. Oh, my two little sisters nearly drove me crazy chanting, "Barbara loves _____!" They would put in the appropriate recipient of my affection that day. But, all-in-all, I count those years as joy.

Growing up is not an easy thing to do.
I decided right off not to take it too seriously.
Why grow up when kids have so much fun.
Why grow up and worry about
saying the right things,
doing the right things,
pleasing the right people.

God,
Let's you and me make a deal.
Don't quit loving me,
And I won't quit loving your world,
and enjoying every minute of it!

WOW! Get a load of that sunset!

Good job, Lord.

"Daddy, you don't understand. God wants me to go to college," I explained.
"Well, then," my dad shot back, "God will have to send you, because your daddy can't."

Alabama Bound

Shortly before I graduated from Shelby County High School, I said, "Daddy, I want to go to college."

"Well, isn't that nice," he said, "but we're not college folks, you know."

"Daddy, you don't understand. God wants me to go to college," I explained.

"Well, then," my dad shot back, "God will have to send you, because your daddy can't."

God did send me. Years before He had asked my best, and I had buckled down. Scholarships and work/scholarships came my way. I didn't get to go to Vanderbilt nor did I get to study medicine, but I did go to the University of Alabama on a fine arts scholarship.

And I went looking. God had something wonderful for me to do. I couldn't be a doctor in Ogbomosho, Nigeria, but He had a place for me to serve. He also had someone to go with me. I tried to call several young men to the foreign missions field while I was at Alabama. Thank goodness, they listened to God and not to me!

My first year at the University was very difficult. Academically, I was prepared, but in every other way, I was not. I became painfully aware of my low estate in life on my first day on campus. The chauffeur of Nancy, one of my hall mates, was carrying in racks and racks of shiny new shoes for her as I arrived. He would not have been able to pack a quarter of those shoes in my three pieces of luggage. I've never forgotten that "out-of-my-league" feeling as I experienced it that day.

I was assigned, as a matter of draw, to the campus beauty

dorm. That was also the dorm where I worked six hours a day. I rang the buzzers for the lines of dates who called on the beauties at Wilson Hall. Any self confidence I had ebbed away in the early days of my freshman year.

I worked so hard at my job and in classes my freshman year that I had not made time for much else. I went to church sporadically since I had to work. Baptist Student Union had not crossed my mind. However, a friend from Columbiana, Ed Rush, unrelentingly kept on me about BSU. "It will mean everything to you," he repeated time after time.

When I returned for my sophomore year, I had made up my mind. I would find another job so that weekends were free, and I would give BSU a try.

"No secretarial job unless you have typing and shorthand," declared the job placement people.

"Would you just give me the name of someone who needs a secretary?" I pleaded.

They confessed later that they gave me the name of someone who would *never* hire me: Annabel Dunham Hagood, the University's illustrious and demanding director of debate. I went directly to Annabel's office and talked her into hiring me, even though I knew not one shorthand symbol. She was so surprised at hiring me, unqualified as I was, that she promptly placed me on the debate squad! The job interview was my try-out.

Where had debate been all my life? I loved it! Miraculously, without any prior experience, my colleague and I won more than 80 percent of our debates that first year. Murray Alley, my colleague, was a terrific debater, and Annabel was the best debate coach in the country. I continued to debate and to be Annabel's secretary all through college.

Also, mostly to get Ed Rush off my back, I gave BSU a looking over. Annabel would say, "Barbara, you can debate or you can do BSU. Choose!"

I refused to choose. I would have given up my classes for either of them, but both were too important to lose.

Debate widened my horizons. Alabama debaters traveled all over the United States. I had been out of state only once before. We stayed in nice hotels and we ate food I'd never even heard of. But the best part of debating was the debating itself. I learned to think on my feet. I learned the value of research. I became a logical thinker.

Annabel was my best sparring partner. She had decided that there was no God. She delighted in trying to burst bubbles for her Baptist debater. She made me examine my faith and stretch to defend it. Finally, I realized God needs no defense. That bedrock has carried me through lots of stormy weather.

Once Annabel confided to me that she wanted to be cremated. I replied, "Oh, Annabel, don't push it. That will come soon enough for you." Compassion is my middle name.

My senior year's finale—the Southern Speech Tournament—was held in Greenville, South Carolina. It was my swan song. I debated before all my heroes—the ones who had written the textbooks I memorized. All six of my judges offered me an assistantship to coach freshman debate at their colleges. I was honored and overwhelmed at being best college debater that year.

Meanwhile, BSU had stretched my spiritual horizons beyond my imaginings. The caliber of leadership in our BSU was phenomenal. Charlie Barnes was BSU director. He and his wife, Flora, became friends and encouragers. Many opportunities were given me to serve. Campus YWA (Young Women's Auxiliary) president was my love. I dreamed of having a YWA in every dormitory at Alabama, but I was told that was not allowed.

"They have everything else under the sun," I pointed out.

"No YWA," the dean repeated.

I went straight to the president's mansion. Dr. Galilee was at home having lunch. No one answered the door, so I walked right into the kitchen.

"Would you have some turnip greens?" he asked, not knowing what else to say.

I accepted, and pleaded my case over lunch. That dear man overruled the dean. We did have YWA in the dorms, and the girls flocked to the meetings.

I had to work summers, so I never had the opportunity to go as a summer missionary. I did help in Bible schools all around Columbiana, and I worked with children in music in revivals. The year I graduated, I was one of the first full-time staffers at Glorieta. I've had a love affair with Glorieta, the Baptist Conference Center in New Mexico, ever since.

BSU became the focus of my social life—a wonderful place for friendships to grow. I fell in love regularly. I was particularly susceptible to Mobile and Baldwin county boys. I also adored Rob James and Leon Gentry. Their talent dazzled me. In fact, I continued to count boys all joy!

But Homer Joiner kept the lines of communication open—and he had my mother on his side. He was in the army stationed at Ft. Gordon, Georgia. Those few weekends and every holiday I was home, he happened to be there, too. He was very handsome in his uniform.

Suddenly, I was graduating.

"Well, Lord," I questioned rather impatiently. "Have you noticed what time it is? I've got decisions to make, and I don't have a clue as to what to do."

Then I made a dreadful mistake. I challenged God, laid down some ultimatums:

"I'll go anywhere you want me to go—except that one-traffic-light hometown of Columbiana."

"I'll do anything you ask—except teach school. Well, maybe college debate, but not high school."

"I'll marry whomever you say—except Homer Joiner. I've told him so a dozen times."

God wants our total obedience. I went back to Columbiana, taught school, and married Homer Joiner.

I discovered I loved all three!

Lord,
I guess it's about time to thank you
That I didn't die of mortification,
Plain, naive country girl
Struggling to survive.

I need to thank you for people
Who looked beneath the surface,
And saw someone made in God's image,
Though the kinship was so dim.

I need to thank you, Lord,
For developing raw talent,
Making me come alive
I can do it! Way to go!

I need to thank you
For showing your face,
Teaching me of your love,
Showing me how to care.

Oh, and Lord,
When the counting is done
Thank you for making it all joy!

Slowly, I returned to Homer who had an I-tried-to-tell-you look on his face. I've seen thousands of those during our life together!

I'll Never Teach School!

I had one week after graduation before boarding the train for a summer at Glorieta. God did some rapid maneuvering during those seven days. My old principal, Woodrow Elliott, was now superintendent of Shelby County schools. He asked me to come to his office; before I left I had agreed to teach "just one year."

Homer was home on leave during that week. "I've applied to be transferred to White Sands Proving Grounds in Alamogordo, New Mexico!" he said. Transferred he was; he left the week that I came home from Glorieta!

He also said, "I know that I've asked you to marry me—several times. When I come home on leave at Christmas, I'm going to ask you one more time. If you say no that will be the last time I'll ask." I knew immediately what my answer would be, but he didn't ask until Christmas!

My brother, Ross, took me to the train station in Birmingham. "Your graduation present will be a pullman ticket," he said. "I'll trade in your regular coach ticket." When he saw the additional price for pullman, he rented a pillow for me. For three days and three nights, I journeyed by coach, sleeping on my pillow.

My BSU director sent me to Albuquerque and wired the folks at Glorieta to meet my train. They did—in Santa Fe. Nobody in the Albuquerque train station had ever heard of brand-new Glorieta. I checked my bag and walked out of the station. It was a strange new world. I walked several blocks, praying every step, and found myself in front of the First Baptist Church of Albuquerque. I walked in and made my way back to the offices.

"Do you know where Glorieta is?" I asked a secretary. She didn't answer. She dashed to the telephone, dialed, and said,

"Thank goodness, Mr. Pat, you haven't left for Glorieta yet. Come by the church."

Mr. Pat, the minister of music, was going to Music Week. I arrived at Glorieta in style.

God had so many joyful experiences for me that summer: staffers I'll never forget, excursions to Santa Fe and to the Indian Pueblos, and Jo Scaggs. Of all the people I met, Southern Baptist missionary to Nigeria, Jo Scaggs, touched me to the heart. I've loved her and prayed for her since I met her.

Then school bells rang. Chelsea Junior High was about 14 miles from Columbiana. I taught all the ninth grade subjects except science. In exchange, I taught eighth grade English. I also had all the junior high girls in physical education.

Thirty students were in my homeroom, and I loved each one. We worked hard, studied hard, and dreamed hard. We had our first school play, the first school annual, and we won the junior high County basketball tournament for girls. It was a cinch. When you learn to dribble and pass around a red-hot wood stove in the gymnasium, you can play basketball! At the end of that first year of teaching, I was hooked!

Homer and I made plans to marry in August and to move to Chelsea. He was officially out of the service, and had decided to go to business college. Since we had only one car, we needed an apartment in Chelsea. Chelsea had no apartments.

"Why don't we find a house we like and see if they just happen to have an apartment," I suggested to an astounded Homer.

We rode around. Finally, I spotted an appropriate home for us. "There!" I said. Homer refused to go to the door with me. A lovely lady answered my knock; I explained our predicament.

Frostily, she replied, "We don't rent rooms."

Slowly, I returned to Homer who had an I-tried-to-tell-you look on his face. I've seen thousands of those during our life together! However, the next day Mrs. Nora Randall came to Columbiana to find me. "Pop and I talked it over; we are rattling around in our big house. You all can have the east wing!"

Homer and I were married August 15, 1954, at First Baptist Church of Columbiana. It was a gorgeous wedding. Records denote that it was the hottest day of the century.

After our honeymoon in Silver Springs, Florida, we moved to Chelsea. Only four months later Mother died; it was decided by the family that we had to move back home.

I taught a second year at Chelsea and then came to Columbiana to teach at my alma mater, Shelby County High School. I brought as many students from Chelsea with me as I could. Part of my bargain to transfer to Columbiana was that I could have one class of debate. The first year, I wanted to observe and not compete. However, by the time we set off for the tournament, I decided maybe we should get a little experience. The little experience that Tommy King and Hoyt Blalock got was winning first place in the state! After that, there was no stopping Shelby High debaters. For the next seven years we won either affirmative or negative first place at the tournament.

Cheerleading was another of my beloved responsibilities. I had been a cheerleader, but I knew nothing about being a sponsor. It took me years to learn. I just knew that "Had a little rooster, set him on the fence . . ." was not a championship yell.

Student council was another fringe benefit that came my way. I didn't mind; the council was composed of our best students. Together we would attempt grand things. But those were extras. I loved teaching, the homerooms, visiting my kids at home, trying to keep them in school. The campus at Shelby High was my missions field. I loved those students with all my heart. I was never Mrs. Joiner to my students; I was always BJ.

Teaching, I discovered years later, is my spiritual gift. It is also my secular gift. I love teaching; seeing my students come alive with ideas thrilled me.

Homer had been working as office manager at Wood-Fruitticher Wholesale Grocery in Birmingham since finishing business school. We bought the sweet old house on Sterrett Street from my dad. He had moved to Texas to seek his fortune. He found her: Ione Dunn. They married and moved back to Columbiana. They bought Uncle Doc Bearden's house next door to us. Ione was the best stepmother in the world.

Life was wonderful except that Homer and I had almost lost hope of having a family of our own. I started graduate work at the University of Alabama. Then several weeks before Christmas, my head started dropping to my desk. I was becoming a most incompetent teacher, I thought, wearily. What I was becoming was a mother!

Prayer for a Student

There was no floor in the house, Lord,
Oh, a few boards here and there
Holding a bed,
a table,
a chair.

She kept her head lowered.
She didn't want me to see her eyes,
the shame,
the pain,
the despair.

Her father was sprawled drunkenly
on the porch.
Her mother, too.
not seeing,
not knowing,
not caring.

Lord, I have to love her extra hard.
Please save her,
Keep her in school,
Deliver her from this.

Oh, Lord, please . . .
Must it be so hard?

Not everybody gets a round of applause for conception!

Honey, We're Going to Have a Baby!

I took a personal leave day, and hardly daring to believe, went to my doctor in Birmingham. He was almost as excited as I was! After an almost-sure confirmation, all I could think about was telling Homer. It was lunchtime, and I knew he'd be at Brittlings' Cafeteria downtown. I ran into a corner drugstore and bought a baby's rattler. Then I plunged into the Christmas shopping crowd at Britlings. There he was. I ran to his table.

"What are you doing in Birmingham on a school day?" he asked.

"I was buying your Christmas present," I replied, shoving the sack into his hands.

I'll never forget the look on his face. "Honey, we're going to have a baby!" I announced to everyone in the cafeteria. Not everybody gets a round of applause for conception!

News spread quickly; the whole student body rejoiced with us. Students carried my books. Cartwheels were curtailed. I developed an irresistible craving for lemons.

Homer put his foot down. "You can finish out the teaching year," he decreed, "but say good-bye to Shelby County High."

My meteoric teaching career was coming to an abrupt halt. My heart nearly broke. But God was preparing a new missions field for me—beginning at home.

School quickly came to a close. The summer was frantic. We prepared a nursery in the Sterrett Street house, and I continued to prepare cheerleaders for competition. We wore off the grass in my backyard. On August 7, we had cheerleader practice. On August 8, I had a baby!

Jacqueline Martin Joiner was born at University Hospital in

Birmingham. She weighed ten pounds and seven ounces! Dr. Barnett congratulated us on our three-month-old baby. She was beautiful. Jackie never went through an awkward age. (In fact, on her first day of kindergarten she had her first marriage proposal and her first kiss—from two different boys.)

When we came home from the hospital, our next-door neighbor, Mrs. Atchison (Atchy), was on the doorstep. She had a chicken pie in her hands and a plea on her lips.

"We don't have Intermediate GA at all, Barbara. You can do that. There's nothing to it."

Atchy continued, "You were a good GA. They could meet at your house." She continued to pursue me as GA leader for weeks. Finally, I agreed to give it a try. So four weeks after Jackie was born, she became a GA. It took me much longer to become an acceptable G.A. leader.

During 1963, I kept a journal of sorts. I was working on several tracks. I planned good, economical menus, I kept records of *everything* happening with Jackie, I noted GA happenings, and I told about discovering mission studies.

I remember well the home mission series for 1963. I can honestly say those studies were life-changing for me and eventually for hundreds in our church. Migrants became real people to me. I hurt for them; I wanted to help them. I taught the adult book, *The Chains Are Strong*, and the YWA book, *The Vacant Hearted* in my home church. Both books covered several groups who need help; I don't know why the migrants pulled at my heart strings but they did. They still do.

In GA regular mission study in *Tell* magazine (now *Accent*), we learned more about migrants. God was softening our hearts so that when the opportunity came to serve, we were ready.

Those GAs were filling up my life as well. Forward Steps had meant a lot to me when I was growing up. I encouraged the girls to work. They did. In the summer, they moved in. Every day my house was filled with a dozen GAs working away. I had two rules. Clean up and be gone by the time Homer gets home. They broke both rules regularly.

The work grew and grew. Coronations became gala affairs. The Queen of England would have been proud to take part.

Then life changed again. I had taken Jackie for her checkup in Birmingham and we'd started home. Going over Red Mountain near the television studios, I suddenly became faint. I'd never fainted in my life, but the world was spinning around. I was terrified for Jackie. I managed to get the car to the side of the highway. I opened the door and was violently sick. Three-year-old Jackie started crying. Coming down the mountain from Channel 13 was Everett Holle, anchor on the local news. Just the week before he had decried people ignoring the cries for help of a woman in New York City.

"Thank you, Lord," I breathed, "for sending a wonderful man to help me."

I waved weakly at Mr. Holle. "Help me," I pleaded.

He waved back at me and drove on.

I was furious! He made me so mad that I stiffened my backbone and vigorously waved down the next set of wheels—a pickup truck. It was so dirty that the driver wrote Homer's office phone number on the grime on the dashboard. Bless you, dear man, wherever you are.

Ten minutes later, Homer roared up. Bob Mullins, my nephew, a medical student at the University of Alabama School of Medicine, lived only a couple of blocks away. Homer was pounding on his door in minutes.

All of them, including Jackie, took me to the emergency room. By that time, I was feeling great and wanted to go home. A very young intern, almost as inexperienced as Bob, solemnly informed me that I had either a brain tumor or a cerebral hemorrhage. What I had was another baby on the way!

That baby continued to deal me a really great time. I had breezed through my pregnancy with Jackie; I was sick every single night I carried Jennifer. I worried incessantly over the little one I was carrying. But on April 9, 1966, the day before Easter, Jennifer McCrary Joiner was born at St. Vincent's Hospital in Birmingham. She was perfect, far from puny at nine pounds and three ounces.

By the way, I shot off the ugliest letter to Everett Holle. He wrote back apologizing. He had thought I was "maybe a little bit inebriated" (like three sheets in the wind). I'm sure I did give that impression. However, I've never watched Channel 13 again—willingly.

Jackie was so proud of Jennifer. She announced at church the next morning that she had a new baby brother and that he was a girl! She called Jennifer Trixie for months. Jackie was happy to have a sister, but she had really wanted a dog.

By the end of the sixties, I was teaching mission studies all over the place. In 1969, I taught the Foreign Mission Study, *Sons of Ishmael*, a dozen times. Little did I dream that in the seventies I would teach some studies more than 50 times! I loved teaching mission studies.

At home, we were trying to teach Jackie and Jennifer about

going to "big church." Homer decided they should get their feet wet going to morning revival services. (While he was at work.)

I took Jackie, along with two biscuits, when she was three years old. She did just fine as long as the biscuits lasted. Mrs. Hatchett observed, "That's what's wrong with the Baptist church today—not enough two biscuit sermons!"

Jennifer was even worse. The first morning she attended, the preacher's subject was Shadrach, Meshach, and Abednego. She had three cats named—you guessed it.

First she said, very loudly, "Why is he talking about our cats?"

I whispered, "I'll explain later."

She did all right until the preacher threw them into the fiery furnace. Then she cried, "No, you can't do that!"

I grabbed her and talked directly into her face: "Jennifer, be quiet. I'll explain later!"

Jen replied, full voice, "Mother, you have bad breath!"

The pastor suggested that I wait a little while on bringing Jennifer into big church.

Life was busy and full and fascinating. Little did I realize what new adventures the Lord had in store for me.

When the world looks dark
And all men seem base,
When troubles keep coming,
Lord, don't hide your face.

Please teach me to hope,
And the meaning of trust.
Please teach me to pray,
And to know that I must.

Just help me remember
The faces of youth.
To think of their living
And walking in truth.

Faces radiant with vision
Hands busy for you.
God, this is your hope
And my hope springs new.

I thank you, dear Master
For letting me be
A leader of youth
For Lord, they lead me!

Written May 15, 1966

*"I tried to think of someone who would appreciate
a robe this ugly, and I thought of you!"*

"God, You Did Good!"

In 1969 I went to my first Alabama WMU Annual Meeting. It
was my sister's fault. Nancy was involved in WMU up to her
ears, serving on the Alabama WMU Sunbeam committee.

Nancy was thoroughly disgusted with me. She'd try to get me
to go to meetings with her and I'd refuse.

"What kind of mother do you think I am?" I'd ask her huffily.
"I have small children, you know!"

"Barbara, you know just enough to be dangerous! You need
to go and get some training. You need to go and get some inspi-
ration!" she'd beg.

Finally, I agreed to go for one day to the Annual Meeting.

Ludie Jones agreed to keep Jackie and Jennifer. I transported
a ton of toys, clothes, and other necessities to the Jones' house.
Then I cried for 15 minutes as I left my two babies. Jackie was
six and Jennifer almost two!

I was big-time late to the meeting at First Baptist Church of
Tuscaloosa. I had missed the pre-session music, the Bible study,
and one missionary speaker before I straggled in. One seat
remained on the top row of the balcony. By the time I reached
"never-never land," Mary Essie Stephens, Alabama's WMU executive director, had made her way to the podium to make the
announcements.

"Before I tell you where lunch will be served (I really was
late!) and where to find the rest rooms," she began, "I have a
burden to share with you."

She reminded the gathering that the year before, in annual
session, they had accepted the challenge given them by their sister state, Pennsylvania.

31

"We agreed to send 100 Baptist Women to Pennsylvania to conduct a telephone survey," she continued. "These women were to locate unchurched people. With these new contacts, the struggling churches could reach out before and during the Crusade of the Americas."

"However," Dr. Stephens said, "the bus leaves for Pittsburgh in three days, and only 25 women have made arrangements to go."

"Twenty-five?" I said to myself, "And you promised 100! What's wrong with this chicken outfit? You all should be ashamed of yourselves!"

Dr. Stephens was still speaking: "The financial requirements are not excessive. Alabama WMU has underwritten chartering the bus. Your fare would be very reasonable. You would spend one night on the road going and coming home, but we have arranged to have four in each room. Your hotel bill would be quite reasonable."

"While you are in Pennsylvania, you would be the guest of the church you are assigned to help. They will house and feed you," she continued. "Let us bow our heads and ask God to call out women from this congregation today."

I bowed my head and helped the Lord. "Send them, Lord, send them," I fervently prayed.

After the morning session, Dr. Stephens looked up in the balcony and motioned to me to come to her. I looked on either side to see the person being summoned.

"You, Barbara," she mouthed the words across the distance. Very slowly I made my way to the front of the church.

"Barbara, Stella White from Clayton cannot go to Pennsylvania. She is a school teacher, and she has the responsibility of her invalid mother. Her mother has been quite ill this year, and Stella has taken all of her sick leave and personal leave days. She wants so much to be a part of the Pennsylvania project, however. So she has come to me to say that she wants to pay your way," she concluded.

I was stunned. I didn't even know Stella White!

"It must be another Barbara Joiner," I finally stammered.

"No," Dr. Stephens said emphatically. "She pointed to you in the balcony and said that she wanted to send you."

"Well, I can't go," I replied, "I have small children, you know."

"You go home and talk this over with your husband," she commanded. "I will call you tomorrow."

When I got home that night, close to midnight, the girls were tucked into their beds and Homer was sound asleep. I could not keep the news! I shook him gently, then harder.

"Wake up, honey," I said, "A woman wants to send me to Pennsylvania!"

"Come to bed," he answered.

I did.

The next morning when Homer woke up, very early, he asked, "Now what is this foolishness about Pennsylvania?"

I explained what had happened the day before. He gave me back my very own words: "You have small children, you know."

"Yes, I know," I replied, "and when Dr. Stephens calls today, I'll tell her it's impossible for me to go."

Homer works in Birmingham. He drives in very early in the morning up beautiful countryside Highway 47, and then on up Highway 280. It's his time to talk to the Lord. When he comes back in the late afternoon traffic he just talks to other drivers.

That morning when Homer went to work, he talked to the Lord. He called me upon arriving at Wood-Fruitticher.

"When Dr. Stephens calls this morning, ask her to give us another day to talk about this," he said. "And don't talk to anybody about this. Well, you can talk to the pastor, but ask him to keep it confidential."

I called our pastor, Raymond Scroggins immediately and told him the whole tale.

"Barbara," he said solemnly, "you must put out the fleece."

"Put out the fleece! There is no time to put out the fleece!" I wanted to cry. I knew about Gideon and the fleece, but I was baffled by what Brother Scroggins meant.

I called Homer.

"I know what the fleece is," he said. "Write down everything you need for the trip . . ."

"That woman is going to pay my way," I interrupted.

"But there are other things needed," he pointed out, "and there's no money for the trip. Make a list of everything you need in order to go. Don't show the list to anybody. Don't go down and nail it to the church door like Martin Luther. Don't even show it to me. Just show it to the Lord. If He doesn't supply every need, we'll know you are not to go."

I still haven't decided if Homer had faith beyond imagining, or if he was certain that God would not supply my needs and that would be the end of that!

Grabbing a pen and paper, I sat down at the kitchen table. The girls were still asleep. My babies! Mercy, who would keep my babies? Someone I would trust! Ten days! Free!

"Forget it!" I said. I knew God did not make free baby sitters!

But I wrote down: "1. Baby-sitter."

Next I went to my closet. I opened the door, then slammed it shut. Ugh! I hadn't taught school in nearly six years. My wardrobe was strictly maternity.

Slowly I opened it again. Hanging on the knob inside the closet door was my robe—a sorry sight. It had weathered two small children. Medicine spots had never washed out. One sleeve was frayed. It was see-through in spots from repeated washings. A robe is low on the necessity list unless you are going to a stranger's house for ten days! I needed a robe.

"2. A robe."

Back to the closet I went. I had several jumpers and a couple of pants suits and one good red dress.

"If I had two good blouses, I could make it," I muttered to myself. Back to the kitchen table I scurried.

"3. Two new blouses."

"What else do I need?" I pondered. Then I remembered. If I went to Pennsylvania I would return on the Saturday before Easter. I had done the Easter shopping: beautiful new dresses, frilly underwear, shiny black patent "Mary Janes" with purses to match. I had even gotten Easter baskets. The girls were ready. That was why there was no money in our bank account!

Except for one thing: I did not have "something special" for Jackie's hair. We had looked all over Birmingham and Montgomery and nothing suited that child.

Reluctantly, I wrote: "4. Something special for Jackie's hair."

Then I knelt down by the kitchen table and started apologizing to the Lord. "I am so ashamed," I said. I was sobbing my heart out when the telephone rang. It was Ludie Jones.

"Barbara, I'm sorry for calling so early, but I just had to tell you the good news. Yesterday the doctor told Clifford that he can go back to work in two weeks."

That was great news! Clifford had been very ill.

She continued, "This morning I was thanking the Lord. I told Him I hadn't done anything for Him in such a long time. I asked Him to send something to my home for me to do. Do you know, Barbara, He spoke right out loud to me and said, 'Ludie, if you'd keep Barbara's children for her, she could do something for both of you!' So, Barbara, will you please go somewhere and do something so that I can keep those precious girls!"

I could hardly breathe! "Oh, Ludie, I'm going to Pennsylvania! Do you want them for ten days?"

"God answers prayer," she said.

I got down on my knees by the kitchen table, "Oh, Lord, thank you," I prayed. "Ludie is the perfect one to keep Jackie and Jennifer. She and Clifford love my girls, and the girls adore them. She'll take good care of them. I won't worry about them. God, you did good!"

I was still on my knees when the doorbell rang. "Mimi," Mildred White Wallace, Columbiana's most colorful inhabitant, was ringing impatiently. Mimi was organist at First Baptist Church of Columbiana. She played that organ like a calliope; most every hymn in waltz-time. She ended each selection with the chords that are commonly known as "How dry I am." Nobody knew how old she was, but she was full of life. She tucked a lace handkerchief in her watchband which she flaunted as she played. She was one-of-a-kind. Everybody adored her.

Mimi had a huge box in her arms.

"Barbara," she said, "My daughter, Beth, gave me this plain, ugly robe for my birthday. It is not the real me." (Later, I saw a real Mimi robe: heavy satin and lace with a feather froufrou around the neck!) Mimi continued, "I tried to think of someone who would appreciate a robe this ugly, and I thought of you!"

She pushed the box into my arms, hurried to her car, and backed down my driveway taking three pieces of shrubbery with her. I went to the bedroom and opened the box. Inside was the most beautiful floor-length, sky-blue robe. It was the loveliest robe I'd ever owned!

Back to the kitchen I went. I couldn't stop the laughter bubbling into my prayer. I knew that God got a kick out of Mimi, too! Then the doorbell chimed again. It was Mabel, one of my sisters-in-law. My sisters and sisters-in-law have given up on me. They are all beautifully coiffed and groomed. They make me walk three steps behind them when we are in public together. One niece is even worse. She has made a public example of my good blue suit because of its longevity. Hopeless people have feelings, too!

Anyway, there stood Mabel with a Penny Palmer bag in her hand, and lovely clothes on her back. Penny Palmer was a very expensive Birmingham store. Mabel had bought a couple of blouses on sale there.

"But you know how much bigger expensive clothes are. The blouses simply swallowed me," she explained.

"I tried to think of someone big enough to wear them, and I thought of you," she said diplomatically. "You can have them if they fit you."

I tried on the two blouses, and they didn't swallow me at all. I had my two new blouses. Immediately I started trying to talk the Lord out of the "something special" for Jackie's hair.

"You don't really have to do that," I said, even as I thanked Him for the blouses.

The doorbell rang again. Opening the door, I faced my friend, Lucy Turner. Jackie had been in her daughter's wedding the summer before. The bridesmaids and the flower girl, Jackie, had all worn ribbon headdresses that were folded over and over and attached to combs. They resembled tiaras and were gorgeous.

Lucy was holding a tiara made of shiny red ribbon.

"What color is Jackie's Easter dress?" she asked.

"Red!" I replied.

"Oh, no," she groaned, "you can't match red to red!"

"Lucy, I guarantee that you have," I stated positively.

And she had.

"My God shall supply all your needs . . ."

And He had.

When I boarded that bus to Pittsburgh 24 hours later, I knew that nothing is impossible for God.

Lord, we say we believe
That the earth is all yours
And everything in it as well.
But Father, those cattle on all of those hills
Belong to somebody else.

We say you made the moon
And the stars in the sky
You made the sun up above to shine.
But Lord, all that money in all of those banks
Belongs to somebody else.

And then on our knees
We call out in fear
We call out in agony.
And the Father pours out all that we need
It belongs to nobody else.

Father, I believe.

The repairman said, "What seems to be the problem?"
"The phone is sticking its tongue out at me,"
I explained.

Pittsburg, Here I Come!

If ever I have felt I was on mission, I did on March 25, 1969, as I boarded the Pittsburgh-bound bus in Birmingham. Arriving at the bus station, Homer and I spotted a woman standing beside the bus sobbing as if she had a broken heart.

I said to Homer, "If we go in pairs, that woman will be my partner."

Sure enough, Arnice Sims from Albertville was my partner. She had every reason to be sad. In the past year she had lost her mother, her husband, and her invalid daughter. She had been their lifeline. Now she felt that her purpose in life was gone. God showed her how needed she was in Pittsburgh as well as back home. Pittsburgh changed her life and mine.

I climbed on the bus and Homer came to the window next to my seat to give me last-minute advice. As we pulled out of the station, he yelled, "Don't get mixed up with the Mafia!"

I laughed and laughed. The Mafia? In Pittsburgh? How ridiculous! All of the women on the bus laughed, too—until we got to Pittsburgh.

What a choice crew that bus held. Our leader from the Alabama WMU staff was Rosie McIntire. I had seen Rosie from afar at the WMU Annual Meeting. Neither of us realized that within months we would become best friends.

Never had I been surrounded by such warm, caring, serving Christian women. I listened and I asked a million questions during that long, first day on the bus. By the time we reached Louisville, Kentucky, my first stop was the local pharmacist. I could hardly make a squeak! My voice was almost gone—and I was going to talk on the telephone.

"What can I do to get my voice back?" I croaked.

"Shut up," advised the pharmacist.

He gave me some medicine, and I did *try* to shut up the rest of the trip.

The following afternoon we arrived in Pittsburgh. Pastors from area churches, from New York, Ohio, and West Virginia were awaiting their telephone operators.

A nattily dressed gentleman with a million dollar smile raced up and down the sides of the bus. "Barbara Joiner! Barbara Joiner!" he called out.

I stuck my head out the window. "Here I am," I said with much trepidation.

"I'm Armando Silverio, the pastor of Rolling Hills Baptist Church. You belong to me," he crowed.

"God help you, Barbara Joiner," pronounced the pastors.

"*No*, God help you, Armando Silverio!" came back the Alabama women.

There's never been another anywhere close to being Armando Silverio, the son of Italian immigrant parents. His father had come to Pennsylvania from Italy to work in the coal mines.

During World War II, Armando had joined the United States Navy and had been sent to Florida. He met Geneva, his wife-to-be, who led him to know Jesus and to accept Him as his Saviour. Together they were serving the Lord in Pittsburgh. Armando had a special way with his Italian brothers and sisters. For Armando, they did most anything.

One day he said to me, "Come, I want you to meet one of the richest men in the city."

We went to a small, expensive candy store. The owner, a charming Italian gentleman, picked out two half-pound solid chocolate Easter eggs for my Jackie and Jennifer. I noted that they cost $16.98 each.

He said proudly, "They are for your little girls—from me!"

I thanked him and asked, "How do you make a living in this small out-of-the-way shop selling such expensive candy?"

"Oh," he said, "Don't worry about me. This is just my front."

God has a superlative sense of humor: I had landed right in the middle of the Mafia!

I've never seen a pastor who loved his people any more than Armando Silverio. I can't forget our trip to an over-look above the city to see the beautiful Golden Triangle where the Monongahela and Allegheny Rivers join to flow into the Ohio.

"Ah, Jerusalem, Jerusalem—Oh, Pittsburgh, Pittsburgh, how oft I would have gathered you under my wings, but you would not," he breathed. Tears were rolling down his face. Mine, too.

I count it all joy that for a few days I worked alongside such a servant of God.

Each of us stayed with a church family. Dr. Glenn Miller and his wife, Margie, opened their home to me. Before the week was over, Margie had become my sister. Daughters, Nancy and Missy, became my buddies.

I walked into the Miller house; Armando led me to the telephone and handed me the telephone book. I was to begin with *G* and go as far as I could. I started calling immediately. The routine was basically the same:

I'd say (in my clearest and most Northern diction), "Hello, this is Barbara Joiner. I'm calling for Rolling Hills Baptist Church. What church do you attend?"

Many said, "St. Bart's." St. Bartholomew was the nearest Catholic church. Others named various churches; some hung up immediately.

I would say to those still on the line, "How often do you attend?" If they answered, "Every week or nearly every week," I'd say, "Good for you!"

If they replied, "Once a year" or "I haven't darkened the door of a church in I can't remember when," I'd say, "I'd like to tell you about my church."

Many listened; some asked for a visit from the pastor. Some were not churched at all. Some were searching.

When I reached the *H*s and the many *Hershey* listings, I hit a bad spot. They were phone-bangers and ugly-talkers. I haven't eaten a Hershey bar since 1969! No matter that the "real" Hersheys live in Hershey, Pennsylvania, not Pittsburgh!

I really got into the phoning. Nancy and Missy brought classmates home from school to listen as I called people. They liked to hear me talk. I met a lot of high school students that week.

Three days into the continuous calling, the phone wore out. In the middle of a call, the phone said, "B-l-l-l-l." It continued to "B-l-l-l-l."

I went next door and called the phone company. The repairman said, "What seems to be the problem?"

"The phone is sticking its tongue out at me," I explained.

"Come on, lady," he snorted.

"Is so! Come on over and see," I said.

He was there in 20 minutes. He picked up the phone and it said, "B-l-l-l-l."

"It stuck its tongue out at me!" he said incredulously.

"I told you so," I reminded him.

He took the phone apart. "It's worn out," he said. "What have you done to this phone?"

"You wouldn't believe it," I replied.

He put in a complete new phone and I was in business again. At the end of the week, I had made more than 2,500 calls—2,743 to be exact.I started early and called late. I felt compelled to do my very best.

I did take off one night for me. Homer's best friend in the army at Ft. Gordon, Georgia, was Chuck Houpt from Valencia, Pennsylvania, a suburb of Pittsburgh. Homer insisted that I get in touch with Chuck and his wife, Marge. They invited me to dinner at their house.

Glenn Miller drove me to Valencia. Chuck and Marge were to bring me back to the Miller's. I took careful notes so that I could navigate on the trip back. Glenn was not so sure I could do it, but I kept insisting that I could.

It was after midnight before we headed back into the city. I guided Chuck without a single wrong turn.

"This is the house," I stated positively. I waved good-bye and ran up the long, winding walk to the house.

I tried the front door. The Millers were going to leave it unlocked for me, but it didn't budge. I knocked lightly, then called Nancy's name. Still no response. Finally, I rang the doorbell. I heard footsteps and the door opened. The biggest man I'd ever seen in my life filled the opening.

"I don't live here," I managed to say.

"No, you don't," replied the man. "Where do you live?"

"Do you know Dr. Glenn Miller who teaches at Pitt?" I asked.

"Sure, he lives four houses down on the same side of the street. Our houses do look alike." he explained.

By that time a lovely black woman had come to the top of the staircase.

"What's wrong, honey?" she asked.

"It's all right. This woman is lost. She's going to Glenn and Margie's. I'd better walk her down there," he added.

"Oh, no, I wouldn't dream of you getting out at this time of night . . ." I protested. But he was already escorting me out of his house. There I was in the middle of the night, walking down the street with a complete stranger in his pajamas and robe!

"You don't sound like you are from Pennsylvania," he probed. "What are you doing here?"

I explained that I was from Alabama and told him about the telephoning.

"You don't sound like a Pennsylvanian, yourself," I observed.

"What are you doing up here?"

He chuckled, "I'm not from Pennsylvania; I'm a Texan. Do you know anything about professional football?"

"I know the Steelers are the Pittsburgh team. Do you play for the Steelers? What is your name?" The questions tumbled out.

"Joe Greene," he replied.

"*Mean* Joe Greene?" I asked with absolute awe!

"Sure am," he grinned.

"I will be a Steeler fan forever," I vowed, "Even though my husband is an absolute fanatic Cowboy fan!"

(Mean Joe, I have been. I even saw you play in the Super Bowl in Miami in 1979. I was there, yelling my heart out as you all beat the Cowboys. You were awesome!)

The week ended too soon, and we boarded our bus to return home with a million stories to tell. God had led us and sustained us in that far land. Pittsburgh had been Holy Ground.

I want to sing out "Holy!" "Holy!"
I want to praise your Holy Name!
To thank you for life's celebrations,
To thank you for comfort in pain.

I want to dance in the streets like David!
I want to praise your Holy Name!
To thank you for wonderful people,
To thank you that Jesus came.

I want to share your blessed message!
I want to praise your Holy Name!
To thank you for life in its fullness,
To thank you for salvation I claim.

I want to telephone a thousand people!
I want to praise your Holy Name!
To tell them a Saviour loves them,
To tell them He's always the same.

Father, I love you.
I want to praise your Holy Name!

"Absolutely not," flung back my friend, "I don't want a bunch of teenagers praying for a husband for me!"

The Ethiopian Love Story

On the bus coming home from Pittsburgh, I spent a lot of time with Rosie McIntire, Alabama's new Acteens director. Once in a long while, maybe even in a lifetime, you meet someone who has always been your friend. That's the way Rosie and I felt about each other. We looked at life in the same way with the same pair of eyes. I found myself listening as Rosie shared about the puzzling things happening in her life.

"I dread planning decision times for Acteens," she confided. "Every service I've been in recently has been tormenting."

"Rosie," I answered, "Maybe God is dealing with you. Maybe He wants you in foreign missions.

"No, not that," she stated emphatically. "I dealt with that in college."

Rosie shared about God's calling her to missions. She told me of going to seminary to prepare, then home to Missouri to fulfill the experience requirement. While serving as GA director for Missouri, she became convinced that God wanted her in WMU.

"No," she said, "God does not want me in foreign missions."

"God called you to foreign missions," I argued. "Perhaps He just thought you needed more than two years experience. *Or,* Rosie, maybe He has somebody for you to go with. Maybe He just now has that person ready to go!"

It's amazing how in tune with the Lord I thought I was!

"Honestly, Barbara," Rosie laughed, "you're just talking silly."

"Rosie, I want my Acteens to become prayer warriors. Why don't you let us pray about your finding God's will for your life?"

"Hmmmm, I don't know." Rosie pondered the request. "Well, I guess so. I really want to find peace about all this."

"And, Rosie, let us pray that if God does have someone for you, He'll reveal that to both of you," I asked.

"Absolutely not," flung back my friend, "I don't want a bunch of teenagers praying for a husband for me!"

"Oh, I'd not put it like that," I promised. "I would do it with dignity." Rosie didn't know me very well or she would never have agreed!

"Keep it dignified," she demanded.

I could hardly wait to get home to share with my girls. They were as excited as I was. On the coffee table in my living room, I kept a stack of missions magazines. Marilyn Hughes was flipping through *The Commission*, the foreign missions magazine, when she squealed, "Here he is!"

Sure enough, in the section on new missionaries, there was Jerry Bedsole. He was from Birmingham, Alabama, unmarried, and on his way to Ethiopia. Jerry was an Auburn University graduate and a veterinarian. He was in missionary orientation at Callaway Gardens, Georgia.

We crowded around Marilyn and her discovery.

"He's cute!" one exclaimed.

"Birmingham!" another said.

"War Eagle!" cried an Auburn fan.

"Let's call Rosie," they begged.

I dialed the number and handed the phone to Marilyn. The girls crowded around, "We found him, Rosie!" they all chimed.

"Put Barbara on the phone!" Rosie demanded. "What's going on? I thought this was going to be handled with dignity! I cannot believe . . ."

"Rosie," I interrupted, "Marilyn really did find him in *The Commission.*"

"Found whom?" Rosie was becoming a bit testy! "Will you please tell me what's going on?"

I took a deep breath. "Well, Marilyn found this single male missionary, Jerry Bedsole . . ."

Rosie jumped in, "I met Jerry. He was appointed at the same service as Maxine."

Maxine Mosely, the former Alabama YWA director, had just been appointed to go to Ghana. She and Rosie were good friends and Rosie had gone to Richmond, Virginia, for Maxine's appointment.

"Well? What did you think of him?" I asked.

"I really didn't pay much attention to him," Rosie admitted. "That was one of the times when the Lord was dealing with me."

"It's simple," I pointed out. "Jerry is over at Callaway and so is

Maxine. Surely you're planning to visit Maxine."

But she didn't—a typical Baptist: she wouldn't visit!

Time kept hurrying by. At every opportunity, I reminded Rosie that orientation would end soon and Jerry would be on his way to Ethiopia. Every Wednesday night, the senior high Acteens prayed fervently.

"Oh, Lord, make Rosie visit at Callaway."

"Dear Lord, bring Jerry to Montgomery where Rosie is."

"Dear Lord, DO SOMETHING!!"

Finally, just weeks before orientation ended, Sherri Hughes prayed, "Lord, if you want Rosie and Jerry together, you take care of it. We don't want this if it isn't your will. We trust you to do what is best." (See how much there is to learn from Acteens!)

I prayed again asking God to take control and did He ever! There was a Young Peoples' Missions Conference scheduled at Shocco. The person in charge got sick. Rosie had to conduct the meeting. One of the missionaries scheduled to come got sick. Jerry Bedsole was sent in his place.

BOOM!!

Rosie called with a brief but soul-satisfying message: "He's great!"

"Get off the phone," I said. "He's going to Ethiopia in two weeks!"

Four dates. That's all the time they had. They discussed the possibilities of their relationship. They had just met and he was leaving in a few days for Ethiopia, the place God had called him. They discussed Rosie's call to missions and her willingness to go. The new relationship had so much potential and yet posed so many questions. "Why did we meet now, so close to Jerry's leaving?" That was the big question.

Finally, they agreed to turn it over to the Lord. They agreed to write and pray.

Rosie went to the airport with Jerry. When he kissed her good-bye, he said, "Remember the next time will be hello . . . and if the Lord is in this, things will happen." Then he boarded the plane and flew away.

They wrote, starting on that day in late August, and the letters continued day after day. They weren't enough. Prayer and aching loneliness showed that. Jerry knew he couldn't live without the girl he had known so briefly and yet had come to love so completely. In October he sent a very special tape, asking Rosie to marry him. She wired back an immediate "Yes!" Her answer, however, was conditional. "Yes," she said, "If I am appointed. Otherwise, the answer has to be no."

46

In record time, appointment procedures were undertaken and accomplished. Finally the day she had been dreading approached. Rosie had high blood pressure. "Nobody with high blood pressure is in any condition for foreign mission service," Rosie reminded herself.

"Pray!" she said to the Columbiana Acteens. And we did.

"Lord, bring down that blood pressure!" That petition went all around the prayer circle—until it came to practical Sherri.

"Lord, we don't want you to bring Rosie's blood pressure down just for tomorrow and have her go to Ethiopia and fall over dead! If you want her to go, bring it down and keep it down"

We all re-prayed our prayers.

"Normal," pronounced the doctor.

"I'm in!" went the message to Ethiopia. "Come home and claim your bride!"

Marriage Climaxes Short Romance of Missionary Couple shouted the news release of the Foreign Mission Board.

On December 30, 1970, Rosie McIntire became Mrs. Jerry Paul Bedsole. Rosie had only two attendants. One was Jennifer Joiner, the proudest, most adorable flower girl in the universe. Fourteen Acteens with smiles of utter contentment looked upon the union with favor and threw rice with wild abandon.

"The age of miracles is not yet passed," they assured each other, but they hadn't seen anything yet!

The Bedsoles reached Ethiopia in 1970. Southern Baptists were involved in a community development program which included public health, agricultural assistance, and vocational training. Jerry and Rosie were part of the Menz highland team. Jerry was the first of the team allowed to share the gospel in an Ethiopian Orthodox church. A cow opened the door!

Columbiana Acteens couldn't just drop the Bedsoles. They decided to send a bull to upgrade the stock in Ethiopia. This was one of Jerry's dreams and Lottie Moon Christmas Offering requests. Working through US Aid, Jerry was able to take the money for one bull and buy seven bulls. Fine cows were produced, not the usual puny ones.

The son of the head priest of the Ethiopian Orthodox church, located across the river from the Bedsoles, bought one of the cows. Jerry visited several times and was there for the birth of a fine healthy calf. All of this led to Jerry's being invited to preach. Other doors began to open to other churches for other members of the team.

In the next few years, Rosie was very busy. Paul was born in

1971, Phil in 1974, and Peter in 1976. Most of her time was spent in being an Ethiopian mama.

While awaiting Peter's birth, complications arose. The Russian doctor at the Black Lion Hospital in Addis Ababa ordered strict bed rest. For weeks I prayed continually for Rosie. Then Jerry called. Peter had been born. Rosie and child were fine, but I couldn't stop praying. For weeks, I continued praying my pre-baby prayers.

I decided that my mind was gone. Then Jerry called again. Rosie had been very ill. He took her to a Seventh Day Adventist Clinic up-country. Peter's delivery had been bungled; Rosie should have died. "Somebody must have been praying," the doctor said.

More dark days were ahead. A military takeover in 1974 had brought turmoil and confusion. By 1977 all Southern Baptist missionaries were out of Ethiopia. Dr. Sam Cannata in his book, *Truth on Trial*, shared the prayer experiences of the mission during his detainment and the evacuation of the Ethiopian mission. The Groces, Beighles, and Bedsoles were the last families to leave in June 1977. All of the mission waited in Kenya to see, if by some miracle, the doors would reopen to their beloved Ethiopia. In March 1978, less than a year after their hasty flight, the Groces returned to Addis Ababa. The Kirklands returned in April, and the Bedsoles returned to Addis in June after a short US furlough.

Trouble struck again in 1980. Rosie had surgery to remove an ovarian cyst; the biopsy showed pre-cancerous cells. The family came back to the States on medical furlough in August. In September surgery was performed again, and all post-op tests were negative. However, the doctor prescribed 12 months of chemotherapy. The 12 months stretched to 18 months. In February follow-up surgery was done. All was well. In June, the Bedsoles returned to Ethiopia.

After years of Communist rule, the Workers' Party of Ethiopia, a Communist party, was officially formed in September 1984. But a more dreaded problem had Ethiopia in its grasp. Some areas had not had rain in three years. Famine and drought tightened their hold. Hundreds were dying daily.

By 1985, thousands were being given dry rations of grain, oil, and dry milk each month through the Baptist mission. In addition, 600-plus were being fed three times daily at the feeding center. By September, 30,000 people were being fed from the Rabel Center alone. Four new feeding centers had been opened to feed over 100,000 people.

The situation grew more desperate the next year. The whole world was praying for rain for Ethiopia. Things could not get worse, but they did. On August 4, 1987, the wonderful, loving business manager of the Ethiopian mission, Troy Waldron, was killed in a helicopter crash. Steve Bartalsky, the Helimission pilot, was also killed. They were on their way to one of the feeding stations. Both were buried in Addis Ababa.

Less than two years later, March 17, 1989, Stan Cannata, volunteer and son of Dr. and Mrs. Sam Cannata, was killed when his pickup truck overturned and rolled down the side of the escarpment on the road to Addis Ababa. Stan had grown up in Ethiopia. His parents had been on the original entry team in the country. He was buried next to Troy Waldron.

In 1990, as I write this book, fighting continues in Ethiopia. The Communist government is no longer in power, but chaos reigns as usual. In the midst of the confusion, Southern Baptists remain, still witnessing of Jesus and His love. Jerry and Rosie Bedsole are the senior members of the Ethiopian mission. The Ethiopian love story continues.

Lord,
Forgive me for not trusting you enough.
You kept prodding
You kept me praying
when I would not
left to my own devices
my own weak faith.

Lord,
Keep me tuned to the needs of my friend.
Wake me up
Trouble my heart
when I would not
left to my own devices
my own weak faith.

I decided that my only hope was to meet Dr. Young before Tuesday morning. I asked God to let that happen. Sure enough, I found myself in the elevator with him Tuesday morning. My tongue cleaved to the roof of my mouth!

Dr. James M. Young, Jr., I Love You!

It all began with *Sons of Ishmael.* I taught that Foreign Mission Study of 1969 a dozen times. Every time I taught the chapter on "Hearing Through Deeds of Mercy," I could hardly wait to get to the part on Yemen! Most people had never heard of Yemen, nor had I, until a daring Southern Baptist doctor, James M. Young, Jr., burst his way into that country in 1964.

Flinging out a map, I'd identify Yemen: in the southwest corner of the Arabian Peninsula, bordered on the north and east by Saudi Arabia, on the south by the South Yemen People's Republic, and on the west by the Red Sea.

The history of Yemen is fascinating. At the time of King Solomon (about 950 B.C.) Yemen and Ethiopia, just across the Red Sea, formed most of the land of Sheba. Spice caravans began their 1,250-mile trip north to Jerusalem from Yemen. One of the seven wonders of the ancient world was the great dam near the capital city of Marib. The Queen of Sheba had her throne in Marib. (Yes, this is the same Queen of Sheba whose trip to see Solomon is recorded in 1 Kings 10:1-13.)

At the time of the Queen of Sheba, Yemen had a high degree of civilization. The great dam was equaled only by the pyramids of Egypt. It watered fields, orchards, and gardens that were the most beautiful in the world. The dam broke about 66 B.C. and was never rebuilt. Today Marib is a small town surrounded by sand and desert and rocks.

Jibla became the capital and remained so until about 900 years ago. Today Jibla has two main points of interest, the 360-room palace of Queen Arwa and the 70-bed Baptist hospital!

Sanaa is the current capital of Yemen. Arabs claim that the

city was first settled by Shem, Noah's son, after he left the ark. It is one of the oldest continually inhabited cities on earth.

From days of glory to 600 years of Turkish captivity, Yemen did not become a nation again until after World War II. In 1912, a dynasty of priest-kings called Imams took over. Even today Yemen is nearly 100 percent Muslim. As long as the Imams were in power, foreigners were kept out of the country. Yemen is a country just now entering the fifteenth century. One authority estimated that 95 percent of the people could not read or write. There were no banks, no paper money, only coins. Travel was largely by foot, donkey, or camel.

In 1962, Imam Ahmed died. The country revolted against having his son take the throne. A republic was begun. At that time, Yemen had been closed to the gospel for more than 1,300 years.

It all began for Jim Young at Ridgecrest Baptist Conference Center. During World War II, Jim had served in the US Navy. He had finished three years of college at Louisiana Polytechnic Institute and planned to get his degree in engineering after the war. He had a little time before school started after he was mustered out, so he decided to give Ridgecrest a look. Jim went unaware that it was Foreign Missions Week. Upon arrival he was given the name of his prayer mate for the week: a young medical missions volunteer.

"I had never considered medicine nor missions before that week," Jim said. "After that, I never considered anything else."

Jim told the Lord that he was willing to go to the country that needed a doctor most or needed a Christian witness most. Little did he realize that both of those needs were wrapped up in the country of Yemen.

Jim finished his schooling and internship. June Buckner became Mrs. Jim Young and four children, Bruce, Mark, Kay, and Jo, were added to their family. They were appointed Southern Baptist missionaries to the Middle Eastern country of Gaza in 1954.

"I do not know when I first became interested in Yemen," Jim says. "But I wanted very much to see what it was like."

He had been in Gaza four years before the opportunity came. He wrote a letter asking for permission to visit. The letter was mailed from Beirut, Lebanon, and while there, Jim visited the Yemini Legation to see if, by some great miracle, he might get a visa to Yemen. He was told that foreigners were not welcome. He wrote the American consulate in Yemen and requested a visa. Nothing happened.

Then came the revolution in 1962. On his first visit to Beirut after the revolution, Jim returned to the Yemini Legation. They gave him a visa! But Yemen was 1,500 miles away and an airline ticket cost almost $500. Then another miracle happened. United Nations' planes were based near Gaza and flew on a regular basis to Yemen. Jim requested a ride, and it was granted.

God continued to open doors. After Jim arrived in Yemen, he was given an appointment with the director general of the Ministry of Health, Ahmed Mohanny. Both men had earned their medical degrees in New Orleans, Louisiana: Jim at LSU School of Medicine, Mohanny in public health at Tulane University. "This almost made us old friends," Jim said.

"Is it possible for us to open a Christian medical mission in Yemen?" Jim asked the director. Mr. Mohanny answered that he welcomed help from any source, even Christian.

So, in September 1964, the impossible became possible as Jim and June Young, their four children, and Marie Luisa Hidalgo, a Spanish Baptist contract nurse, moved to Yemen. In March 1965, the temporary Baptist clinic in Taiz began seeing patients. During the first month, they saw almost a thousand patients in over 1,300 clinic visits.

In 1966, they moved to their present location, Jibla. Working in trailers while the Jibla Baptist Hospital was being built, they saw 17,000 patients during that year. One year later, the new 70-bed Baptist hospital opened its doors.

Patients flock to the hospital from all over Yemen—from the Saudi Arabian border, from the Red Sea, from Aden. They travel by foot or by donkey. When they reach a road, if they can get a ride, they continue by car. Jim tells of one woman who had to walk 15 days, already weak and sick, to get to the hospital.

John D. Hughey, former Foreign Mission Board secretary for Europe and the Middle East said, "That a Baptist witness could be begun in a country almost 100 percent Muslim and that a hospital could be constructed and equipped under such unfavorable conditions seem beyond the realm of possibility. But the impossible has become a wonderful reality in Yemen."

I read everything I could find about Yemen. I prayed for the work, for the missionaries. New missionaries went to Yemen and I rejoiced. I loved Yemen and I was a tremendous admirer of Jim and June Young.

The first WMU annual meeting I attended sent me to Pittsburgh. I was asked to report on Pittsburgh at my second meeting.

"Oh, I can't do that," I protested to Hermoine Jackson, the program committee chairman.

"Of course, you can, Barbara," she stated emphatically. Hermoine always made me believe I could do anything. "You will speak for twenty minutes on Tuesday morning—right before Dr. Young."

"Dr. Young who?" I asked breathlessly.

"Dr. James M. Young, Jr." she replied.

"Dr. James M. Young, Jr., from where?" I babbled.

"Dr. James M. Young, Jr., from Yemen. Do you know him?" she inquired.

"Yes!" I shouted. Then I added, "I *feel* like I know him . . . no, I don't know him personally . . . oh, my goodness. I can't! I cannot follow him on program! I will be a wreck!"

By this point I was making no sense at all. Hermoine was hysterical with laughter.

I decided that my only hope was to meet Dr. Young before Tuesday morning. I asked God to let that happen. Sure enough, I found myself in the elevator with him Tuesday morning. My tongue cleaved to the roof of my mouth!

I asked the Lord to help me keep my mind on Pittsburgh. He did, and I shared about our wonderful trip. I did not look at the front row where Dr. Young was sitting, waiting to address us. When I finished, I walked down the steps to sit on the front row. Dr. Young rose, took my arm, and escorted me to my seat. As he did, he said, "I hate to follow you."

I could not believe my ears! Then I sat down where he had been sitting, and it was still warm! I wanted to build a tabernacle! I had a king-size case of hero worship.

At the luncheon for program guests following the morning session, Jim Young and I became friends. Less than a month later he visited Homer and me in Columbiana and spoke to our associational Acteens. Those Acteens greeted him with enough adhesive tape and hypodermic needles, both desperately needed in Yemen, to fill three huge oil drums.

Since then the Youngs have been our house guests several times. Our whole family have been prayer supporters. When Alabama friend, Dr. Martha Myers, became a Yemen missionary, our bonds with Yemen became stronger. When I stood many years later with Martha in front of Jibla Hospital, tears flooded my eyes. I would never have dreamed as I taught *Sons of Ishmael* that someday I would stand in that holy spot.

Dr. James M. Young, Jr., I love you. You, too, June. You make me proud to be a Southern Baptist.

First Night in Yemen

Exhausted but excited I finally fell asleep.
All I'd seen in Yemen
Flickered through my dreams.
How I loved this storied land
How long I'd prayed for her.
Then through the silent darkened night
The muezzin's cry rang out.

Oh, yes, I'd prayed and studied hard.
I had taught,
And spoken much.
I knew this land was dark in sin,
That Allah held her tight.
Then through the silent darkened night
The muezzin's cry rang out.

My heart stood still, my blood ran cold.
I shivered
'Neath the sheet.
I felt the bonds that bound her soul,
The weight of Islam's chains.
When through the silent darkened night
The muezzin's cry rang out.

She sobbed, "It's all up here in my head, but it's not in my heart."

Migrant Camp—the Beginning

Since Alabama WMU Annual Meetings were such life-changing events for me, I should have been wary when I journeyed to Mobile for my third meeting. Instead, I went gladly, expecting something wonderful to happen. I was not disappointed. I heard and met Gerald Blackburn, director of missions for Baldwin Association across the bay from Mobile.

God had prepared me to hear Gerald. Some years before I had taught the Home Mission Study books *The Chains Are Strong* and *The Vacant Hearted*. Both books had targeted groups with major needs, but the group that captured my attention were the migrants. Someone has said that migrants are the invisible people. They surely had been invisible to me, but when I read Jacqueline Durham's story about a little girl named Reney in *The Vacant Hearted*, they became very real to me. I had no idea what a vital part of my life they would become.

When Gerald presented the needs in Baldwin Association, my heart burned to help meet those needs. Boldly, I accosted him at the end of the session. "Mr. Blackburn, I work with senior high Acteens at First Baptist Church of Columbiana. Could we come help with the migrants? We could teach Bible school, do anything that needs to be done."

The look on his face said, "All I need is a bunch of giggling teenagers." He made a polite reply; we went our separate ways.

Several months passed; the phone rang and Gerald said, "Are you out of school the last week of May?"

Usually we are not but that year, school was ending earlier! "Yes!" I cried.

"Well, our associational camp is vacant that week. If you'd

like to bring your Acteens to help with the migrants, you may."

We had to clean the camp which had been unused all winter and do our own cooking, but we were in! We slaved getting ready. We were determined to do the best job we could.

Just 13 went, including my eight-year-old Jackie and four-year-old Jennifer. None of us had ever seen a migrant, but from the beginning, God gave us great eagerness and a deep love for these people. (During the 20 years we've gone to migrant camp, neither of those attitudes has changed.)

God went before us. He gave me a special friend the very first night we went into the camps, Aledia Garcia. She and her husband, Miguel, had 11 living children. She felt sorry for me since I had only two.

"Maybe God will give you another one," she sympathized.

"Maybe not," I quickly replied, "I'm having a hard enough time raising two!"

Aledia recognized that I needed help. She unplugged lights in the meager rooms of the camp and plugged in our lights. She rounded up the children. She opened her own room for the adults to come for Bible study. I loved her that first night and have continued to through the years. Our time together was too brief. Her family joined the Sugar Beet trail after three years. Every year I look for their return to Alabama, hoping.

Aledia's youngest was a precious 4-year-old named Lydia. She and Jennifer became fast friends. Her oldest was 17-year-old Miguel, Jr., who was the star pupil of the youth class.

We worked in only two camps, both in Summerdale, separated by a barbed wire fence. It was a glorious week. We learned a lot more than the migrants did.

Jennifer taught her mother and Aledia several truths that have sustained me over the years. I made sure every night before we left Baldwin Baptist Camp that *everybody* (especially Jackie and Jennifer) went to the bathroom. There was no way I would have my daughters visit the "hole in the floor." Third night out, here came Jennifer, walking cross-legged. Before I could scream or faint, Aledia said to her oldest daughter, Seprianna, "Take this baby to the bathroom. Hold her up. Be careful."

Then Aledia turned on me, furious. "Why did you bring your little ones down here? They are not used to all this dirt and insects. They could get very sick!"

I said, "I know that, Aledia. It scares me to death, but I've asked God to keep them from sickness. I wanted to come and tell you about Jesus so much, and I had no one to keep them, so I had to bring them with me."

I could see the change taking place in her heart. I was no longer goody-two-shoes, but a friend willing to come at great cost. God has been faithful; He has protected my daughters and all the rest of us for over 20 years. I've cringed many times when I've seen Jackie or Jennifer sharing a tortilla filled with beans with one of their migrant friends. But the "episootis," my mother's word for all things terrible, never came!

Jennifer also taught me why we were ministering to migrants. Her friend, Lydia, was crying when we arrived at the camp one night. Jen bounded from the van and ran to her. "What's wrong, Lydia?" she asked.

Lydia didn't answer; she continued to cry and hold her hand just below the hairline of her gorgeous black hair.

"Did Pepeto hit you?" Jen demanded. Pepeto hit everybody, including Jen until she hit him back a whole lot harder.

Finally, Lydia took her hand away and held back her hair to reveal a huge boil, fiery red. Jen reacted like any four-year-old: "Yuck!" But after thinking a minute, she said to her friend, "Don't cry, Lydia. Come on over here to my mama. She'll take our picture, holding hands, being friends."

That picture is one of my treasures. It shows a long-legged blonde child sandwiched between two raven-haired, black-eyed little migrant girls. They are holding hands, squeezed up together. Lydia is still holding that hurtful boil, but she's smiling and hanging on to her friend.

That picture also tells my philosophy of migrant work. We can't do much about the boils—the horrible living conditions, the hazardous health problems, the low wages—but we can hold hands and be friends. Even more important, we can introduce them to our best friend, Jesus.

Another major event took place that first year. Aledia's oldest son, Miguel, came to me with a special request. He had finished his junior year in high school. More than anything he wanted to complete high school. However, his uncles had decided he was old enough to drive a truck full time.

"Would you talk to Mama?" he pleaded.

I assured him that I would but only after praying that night and asking the Acteens to pray also.

The following night I went into the camp ready to talk to Aledia. "Aren't you going to be proud when Miguel graduates from high school?" I began. "Is he the first in the family to graduate? He is such a fine young man, so bright, the smartest one in the youth class."

Aledia kept nodding her head as I chattered away. Then she

burst out, "He is smart, my Miguel; he deserves to graduate."

I knew then that those uncles didn't have a prayer. Migrant mothers love their children and want a better life for them. Aledia knew, as most migrants do, that there are only two ways off the migrant trail. You die, and they do that far too often and far too young, or you get an education. She was determined for Miguel to have an education and a chance.

I gave the Acteens the high sign: it's going to be all right for Miguel! We finished that Friday night with piñatas and health kits and lots of hugs and kisses.

We went back to Baldwin Baptist Camp to celebrate. Every night we had gone down to the pier to share and pray together. We did so with thanksgiving that last night. We had made it! God has used us! No decisions had been made by the migrants, but many seeds had been planted. And we'd be back. Oh, yes, we would be back.

Going up from the pier, suddenly Cindy Rasco sank to the ground in the middle of the sea grass. Those closest to her rushed to her side.

She sobbed, "It's all up here in my head, but it's not in my heart."

"It doesn't have to be," Jeanie Turner said, hugging her, "just let Jesus come into your heart."

Four of us huddled on the banks of Wolf Bay, arm-in-arm. We prayed for the Lord to come into Cindy's heart. All at once, she gasped, "He has! I felt Him come in. Thank you, Jesus!"

Have you ever experienced the presence of the Lord in such an exhilarating way that joy floods the room, or the patch of grass, where you are? I believe He longs for that to be a daily experience as we walk and talk with Him and as we walk among our brothers and sisters sharing His love.

I count every hot, dirty hour in migrant camps all joy!

I sit playing with children who are not mine,
Nor do they belong to people
that I have anything in common with
except a few English/Spanish words.
Yet I have rarely if ever
felt closer to any children.
The beauty of God's work shines out at me,
sparkles in black eyes
And for once I understand the meaning
of the words
IN HIS IMAGE.

Lord, it is so easy to care
while I am living with them.
Don't let me grow cold and forget them
when I return to my air-conditioned home,
my clean school.
Never let me forget that they are here—
That they are my brothers—
and my brothers are my responsibility.
Amen.

Written by Joe Smith, First Baptist Church youth at migrant camp in 1980. Joe is now associate pastor/administration, Broadway Baptist Church, Fort Worth, Texas.

"Barbara, don't get down on your knees. Just Anglos do that."

Our Lady of the Potatoes

When we returned to migrant camp the second year, we felt a hundred years wiser. We knew better how to prepare, and we were going back to friends, not strangers. We had no idea that turnover in migrant camps is phenomenal, and little did we suspect what waited for us.

We went to the same two camps in Summerdale. However, the reception was *not* warm and welcoming. It was the year of the *BIG* potato crop. Every man, woman, and child was working unbelievably long hours. The best potato pickers, all 13 of them, were still in Weslaco, Texas, attending the graduation ceremonies for Miguel Garcia, Jr.

My name was mud. The crew chief, Benito Rodriguez, would stride out when the last truck pulled in, and he'd glare at me as if I were public enemy number one. I couldn't blame him for being angry with me, but it made me mad that he infected the whole camp with his hatred. The children were terrors and they had been angels the year before. No adult came to Bible study. They were working so hard.

On the other side of the barbed wire, the other camp was going great, in spite of the big crop. Every night as we traveled to Summerdale, migrants would stop and ask us to come to their camp to tell their children Bible stories. By Wednesday, I was worn down. I decided that we would go to another camp for the last three nights. No use wasting our time. I waited for Benito Rodriguez to get in from the fields. He stomped toward me in his huge cowboy boots. He scowled down at me.

"You think you understand my people," he charged, before I could say a word.

"No, Benito," I replied, "I don't claim to understand you, but I do love all of you."

He had not expected that reply and he didn't like it. He scratched off in his boots and started again. I knew what was coming.

"You think you understand my people," he began, "but you won't understand them until you work beside them in the field!"

Kill the interfering woman, that was his strategy. She can't stand the brutal heat and punishing labor in the potato fields.

He was right, of course, but he didn't know that I'm not a quitter. He didn't know that I realized that our integrity, our right to come to migrant camp was on the line. Most important, Benito had no idea that God was heavily involved.

I told the Acteens nothing until we got to the sharing time on the pier. After explaining the situation I said to them, "Can you all handle everything at Baldwin Baptist Camp during the day tomorrow, including Jackie and Jennifer?"

I could see the concern on their faces, even in the moonlight. They began to speak, assuring me of their support and their prayers. Then my niece, Vicki Joiner asked, "Where do we send your body?"

"Oh, Vicki, I'm not going to die! But can you all handle all the preparations for tomorrow night?" I pressed.

They assured me that they could. We prayed a long time that night. I must confess I talked with more courage than I possessed. I never did get to sleep. I had a million questions. One loomed larger than the others. I knew I couldn't drink out of the slimy green water jug, but neither could I hurt their feelings. Just like me to worry about trivial matters in the face of heat stroke!

Benito had ordered me to be there before sunrise; I was. The teenagers were waiting for me. Somehow they knew what had happened. They hauled me up to a good place on the back of the truck, next to the cab. All the way to the field they told me how to pick up, how to stack my baskets, dozens of details. They were openly defying their crew chief. I worried about that.

When we reached the fields, the tractor started rolling, digging up the potatoes and sending billows of choking dust right on us. Benito marked off the skips (a length of the row) each picker was to work. My skip was long. The teenagers flew to my defense. I didn't understand Spanish, but I knew they were arguing that my skip was too long. Benito strolled on, smiling.

We started filling our baskets. A good crop means a fast basket. I kept pace, row after row. The teenagers flashed smiles of encouragement. The sun beat down; rivers of mud rolled down my face. I prayed a lot; I could feel the prayers of the Acteens and my two little girls. Around ten o'clock my back began to feel as if it would break momentarily. I thought about getting down on my knees. Could I keep up?

Valentino, one of my favorites, said, "Barbara, don't get down on your knees. Just Anglos do that."

My heart soared. Accepted! I was one of them, at least in Valentino's book. I would not sink to my knees. Stiffen, back, we've got miles to go before we sleep!

Lunchtime came. I had wrapped a piece of toast and a couple of slices of bacon in a piece of foil. I dug it out of my pocket. It looked pitiful but tasted wonderful.

The water jug made its way to me. "Don't tempt me," I said, "If I ever start drinking water, I'll never pick up another potato." As I passed it by, my tongue was stuck to the roof of my mouth.

Benito came by while we were eating. "You're keeping up, aren't you?" he observed.

"Yep," I said.

Back to work. It got hotter in the afternoon. Around two o'clock I decided it would be better for me to go ahead and die. We had reached a row bounded by the highway. The tractor had crossed the highway and was waiting for us to clean the last row and cross over. As we picked, a big luxury car drove down the road and stopped in the middle of the teenagers. The windows glided down. The car was filled with Anglo teenagers.

As one they jeered, "Hey, you dirty migrant kids!"

My migrant friends didn't miss a beat. They kept on throwing potatoes in their baskets. My heart broke. I knew they had received such taunts before, but I had not. And those kids were white—like me. Of course, they couldn't tell; I was covered with grime from head to foot.

So I rose, like an avenging mother, and looked them in the eye, "Hey, you dirty white kids." And they were dirty—on the inside where it counts. That put some iron in my backbone. The migrants didn't say a word, but I felt their love absolutely flooding the field. We picked on.

Benito checked again. "Doing good," he chortled. "I guess I'd better hire you on."

"I believe I can find a nicer crew chief," I announced.

He threw back his head and laughed. The wall was beginning to look less formidable.

At four o'clock the tractor broke down. God knew I had had it. He just zapped that tractor in its tracks. In my heart I sang "The Doxology" over and over.

63

Benito came by and said, "You'll have to stay until Saturday to collect your check."

"Can't," I replied. "But I'll leave a note for Miguel to tell him to collect my check for his graduation present."

"You worked all day in the blazing sun for a Tex-Mex kid?" he asked. He knew very well that more was at stake than Miguel.

"He's not just a Tex-Mex kid; he's my friend and I'm proud of him," I said.

A big grin came over Benito's face, "I'm pretty proud of him myself," he said, "he's my nephew."

"Your nephew? How can a sweet kid like Miguel have a bear of an uncle like you?" I bellowed.

Benito threw back his head and howled. I saw the last brick in the wall come tumbling down.

When the accounts were done at the end of the day, Alvaro Marino, the best picker in the camp that year, had picked up 97 baskets in that short day. I was close on his heels with 87.

It was Benito's mother, Filipito, who gave me the name that has lingered on in migrant circles: Our Lady of the Potatoes. For one day, I really was Our Lady of the Potatoes. The God I love and serve is Lord of the mountains, and Lord of the sea, and surely He is Lord of the potatoe fields. I'm living proof!

Father,
How can you just sit there
When tiny babies in cardboard boxes
are carried to the fields
and swelter in the sun?

Father,
Have you noticed rats?
They scurry in dark corners
where children sleep
on filthy wooden floors!

Father,
Did you see the tiny mound—
Food for a family of nine?
bloated stomachs rumble
as we try to teach of love!

Now Lord,
I'm doing all I can,
But they need so much!
Oh . . . mostly they need you?
Forgive me, Father,
I have the questions.
You are the answer.

How do you measure 21 years of migrant camp? Is it by gallons of drink mix and dozens of cookies served? Early on we measured one year: 75 gallons of drink mix and 2,000 cookies.

We Haven't Been the Same Since

We left migrant camp in 1971 on top of the world. The migrants, and especially Benito Rodriguez, the crew chief, had opened their hearts to us. Benito's mother, Filipito, had cooked a huge wash pot full of homemade tamales in fresh corn shucks for the entire camp and us. We knew we'd be welcomed back the next year.

Sure enough, in 1972 we arrived in Baldwin county to many hugs and kisses. The Garcia family was back. In fact, both of our old camps were intact. We had a glorious week of teaching; the migrants were beginning to understand and respond.

We returned to Columbiana bubbling over with joy, but tragedy soon struck. Most migrants in Baldwin county leave after harvesting the potatoes to go to the Sand Mountain area in North Alabama to pick another potato crop. The trail comes through Shelby county; Columbiana is the county seat.

On June 17, 1972, the truck carrying the massive potato grader, most of the possessions of an entire camp, and six migrant men went over the mountainside, crashed, and burned.

Charles Stroud, our pastor, described the horrible event in our church newsletter.

"Mission challenge was thrown in our laps this week when a terrible wreck in Shelby county took the lives of five migrant workers: Manuel Barrera, Leandro Barrera, Romigio Sanites, Oseara Conneara, and Luiana Chapa. Jose Dominguez is hospitalized in critical condition.

"Practically all of the personal belongings of the whole work crew, men, women, and children, were in the wrecked truck. There was some salvage from the wreck.

"Within the space of a few hours, Columbiana people made a tremendous response to the needs. So much was being done and so many people were involved that it would be almost impossible to name them. The Lord knows who served and who gave, and each will be rewarded by Him.

"Amazingly, it was some of the same migrant families who had been served by our Acteens in Baldwin county for the last three years. Therefore, the Acteens and their leaders spearheaded the effort. But contributions of all kinds and amounts were received from people of all religious faiths.

"Our appreciation and deep gratitude are expressed to everyone who participated in missions in our own front yard."

The call came from one of the directors of missions in North Alabama. "A truck has not shown up," Brother Pope said. "Have you heard anything?"

Within the hour I heard the worst. Manuel Barrera, the crew chief in one of our camps, his son, Leandro, and three others had died in a fiery crash. Jose Dominguez was missing. All of these men and their families were in the Summerdale camp across the barbed wire from my camp. Acteens leader, Peg Hill, and seven Acteens had worked with them for three years. All of us were devastated.

Our church sprang into action. Some of the men went to the wreck site and brought back the battered remains of the migrants' possessions. Many people brought in bedrolls, linens, hot plates, pans, dishes, and other needed items.

When some of the migrants came to retrieve what was left of the potato grader, they found a church packed with gifts for them. They also found men, women, and Acteens with hot coffee, sandwiches, and cake. It was a dismal day; rain was pouring. We brought the broken men into the church kitchen and fed them and waited on them with love. They were overwhelmed.

People flooded to the funeral home in Columbiana to comfort the familes. Homer located Jose who had been carried to a Birmingham hospital. As he healed, many were faithful to care for his needs.

Through the years the story of the Alabama wreck has become a part of migrant folklore. And the benediction has always been: "What a terrible thing to happen, but, thank God, it happened where people care."

The fourth year of migrant camp was revolutionary. The senior high boys had been demanding equal rights for years. My reply was for them to find a man to ride herd on them and they were in. In 1973, Tom Stoker, the big Texan, came to be our minister of music. So, the Pioneer Royal Ambassadors who went through the migrant camp training, went to Baldwin county. The additional help meant that we could go into more camps—four. It was Jackie's first year to teach. At age 11 she could handle a group of preschoolers with one hand behind her back!

In 1975, a drastic change came in potato harvesting. Machines were available to dig and load eight rows of potatoes at one time. Field workers found themselves with little work. Shed workers, however, were laboring night and day. Migrants had to take time off for Bible study. Children were free to come. We continued to go to Baldwin county and our Bible schools grew, to our amazement.

David Hedden came into our lives that year. He had grown up in Baldwin county but had never been involved with migrants. He was working at Baldwin Baptist Camp during the summer and agreed to be "wheels" for one of our camps. At the end of the week David said, "A great man once said: 'Why are you so anxious to see God with your eyes closed? See Him with your eyes open—in the form of the poor, the starved, the illiterate, and the afflicted.' Truly you have seen God this week. Keep the vision." David worked with us two more summers, then went to Brazil as a summer missionary, then on to seminary. Now he and his wife, Cindy, serve as Southern Baptist home missionaries in Georgia.

Migrant camp can also claim home missionary Ray Joiner as one of its own. Ray was one of the guys pushing for equal rights when the boys first got to go to Baldwin county. Look where it got him: right in the middle of the inner-city gangs! He is director of Birmingham Baptist Center.

Two other migrant camp alumni are part of the foreign missions team. Dr. Martha Myers and Dr. Ron Murff brought their little black bags and Bibles while in medical school and as interns to help the migrants with physical and spiritual needs. Martha is now doing the same thing in Yemen, Ron in Rwanda.

How do you measure 21 years of migrant camp? Is it by gallons of drink mix and dozens of cookies served? Early on we measured *one* year: 75 gallons of drink mix and 2,000 cookies. In 21 years that comes to 1,575 gallons of *red* drink mix and 42,000 cookies. Is it by health kits given? We think over 10,000. By Bibles and tracts? More than 20,000. By the number of migrants taught? At least 5,000. By the number who have accepted Christ? Over 100 at this point.

But the intangibles far outweigh the things that can be measured. Some of these are expressed in the WMU Watchword from several years ago. My paraphrase of 2 Thessalonians 1:3 (Phillips) reads like this: "My brothers (and sisters) I thank God for you. Your faith has made such strides and your love toward one another (and toward migrants) has reached such proportions that we actually boast about you . . . because you have shown such endurance (through cold showers, backed-up sewage, hot humid weather, yellow flies and mosquitoes) and faith (that shed workers really would come in and that migrants would come to know the Lord of Lords)."

David Hedden said it best: Baptists in Baldwin county bought some land down on Wolf Bay and they built a pier. Then folks from Columbiana started coming down and filling that pier and Baldwin county hasn't been the same since.

We haven't been the same either.

Soliloquy of a Migrant Mother

Source Unknown

Oh, God——are you there?
If you are, the man said you'd hear.
I don't know how to pray, but I'll try.
There must be a way
To let you know that things are hard.
The way's so long and dreary.
Weariness fills all my soul.
The ache in my back is worse.
I stoop, stoop, stoop.
Cherries will be easier.
No stooping, only reaching.
Then I can see the sky.
God, do people eating beans know how
hard they are to pick?
When we get to cherries maybe
I can pray a little better.
Looking up, I'll try to remember
How You care. The man said
You care so much.
Your Son is dead.
But he also said
He is alive again.
. . . Strange . . .
I can't think how that would be.
Tomorrow we go.
The man said
You'd go all the way with us.
Don't let the truck break down again.
He said, "Believe." But how?
I'm so tired now.
Tomorrow I'll try to remember how he said it was.

Never has a book burned within me; not even an article has flickered.

The Saga of the Deadly Deadlines

I've always despised deadlines. In high school, and more so in college, assigned papers shriveled my soul. While teaching, I wrote when I had to. I cut and constructed stories, even Shakespeare, for class recitations. I wrote skits for the cheerleaders. The debaters and I hammered out debate cases. Later, Acteens skits and plays were added to my chores.

Never has a book burned within me; not even an article has flickered.

WMU slipped up on my blind side. In 1970, Rosanne Osborne, the editor of *Royal Service*, asked me to do a portion of "Woman Aware." This feature, which I wiped out single-handedly, posed a problem which was explored by an expert in the field. Then three typical Baptist Women made a brief (300 word) response and gave their solutions to the problem.

The problem I was asked to examine was the plight of the migrants. We had worked with migrants for two years by that time. I was totally, completely in sympathy with them. I had something to say, I thought.

I accepted the assignment. Rosanne sent Beth Hayworth's brilliant essay on migrants. I dove into it with all my energy and fabulous experience (a little over two weeks of actually working with migrants).

Two other Baptist Women were working simultaneously on their replies. They were by no means typical Baptist Women! Their replies showed their broad experiences, their immaculate educational credentials, and their unmitigated writing abilities. Jane Allison from Knoxville, Tennessee, and Mary Foster from Greenville, South Carolina, wrote concise, intelligent replies. My reply was rural, illiterate, and emotional. I was mortified when my June 1971 *Royal Service* arrived.

I had a theory that women only read "their part" on page 12 and the prayer calendar. Trusting this theory, I told no one in my church to pray for me. Sure enough, nobody in my church read the feature. No one said a word about "Woman Aware."

Comforted that no one had read pages 14 and 15 except Jane, Mary, and me, I went on my merry way to migrant camp.

The first day down in Baldwin county, the phone rang. It was the wife of a local pastor.

"May I come over?" she asked.

"Sure," I said, suspecting nothing.

When she arrived, she said, "Do you remember the article you wrote for *Royal Service* this month?"

Oh, my word! I had talked about the lack of concern of local churches, the closed doors of local churches . . . I was dead in the water!

"Well," she said, "you are right. I took a group on our old church bus to the nearest camp. It was less than ten minutes away. I read your article to them; we voted to have Bible school in the camp. Eight migrants came to know the Lord! We've been sending our bus every Sunday to bring the migrants to services in our church, and we'll keep on doing this."

Tears were running down my face. "Ramona, I've worried about that article being dumb, but if it opened the doors to one church, I could care less what any nitpickers might say!"

I credit Ramona Wentworth for my continuing to write. It certainly wasn't the money. I still have the receipt for my first WMU article: $4.50!

It came as a complete shock when I was invited to a writers conference at WMU, SBC. I met Alma Hunt and Marie Mathis, the WMU executive director and president. I also met Jane Allison and Mary Foster. They were as intelligent and sophisticated as they sounded on paper. We became fast friends, three rookie writers. We've prayed each other through a lot of writing assignments since then.

All of us who have written for the missions magazines owe a tremendous debt to the gifted editors who have taught us. I was fortunate to have the best at the beginning, Rosanne Osborne and Adrianne Bonham. There may be better teachers of writing skills, but I doubt it. All I know about writing, they taught me. Since then, I've had wonderful editors to guide me and encourage me. I am very grateful.

At that first conference Alma Hunt and Marie Mathis were

keynote speakers at an elaborate banquet. They put the weight of missionary education for 1972 and 1973 squarely on our shoulders. I left feeling as if I had the whole world on my back. Jane Allison and I walked back to our hotel.

All at once Jane blurted out, "When are your issues in *Royal Service?*"

"January, February, and March 1973, Current Missions," I replied.

"Oh, no," Jane moaned. "I have October, November, and December 1972 Current Missions. That's six months down the drain!"

WMU survived those six months in spite of our grave reservations. Jane and I, and Mary as well, continued to write. The next year all three of us were invited back to writers conference.

In addition, Stuart Clavert came that year. God had led my best friend, Rosie Bedsole, to Ethiopia. I needed a best friend in the US, so God sent Stuart. Since then, we have had many wonderful experiences. We have been roommates at Shocco and Ridgecrest, as well as lots of state meetings. Stuart has gone with our Acteens Activators to New Mexico, Massachusetts, Jamaica, and Minnesota. She's prayed me and my family through many things, and I've done the same for her and her family. I thank God for her and for our friendship.

New friends sweetened the agony of deadlines, but the wild experiences I have had writing have doubled the agony!

Dr. Merrill Moore was an old friend from Glorieta days. I knew he would send me a good tape when I had a writing assignment on medical missions in the Middle East. He was serving in Gaza.

Sure enough, his tape came promptly. I tested it and heard him say, "Hello, Barbara. Hope this tape is what you need."

I stored the tape away and waited for material from Yemen, Jordan, and India to arrive. Finally, well before my deadline, fat letters arrived from Jim Young in Yemen and Rebekah Naylor in India. I waited some more. The deadline was fast approaching. I put the Gaza tape in the player and had pen and paper ready to decipher.

Imagine my absolute horror when after Merrill's "hello" the tape lapsed into Arabic. Off I ran to the University of Montevallo. I knew several foreign students there who spoke Arabic. All the way to the school, I kept saying, "This is not funny, Merrill! I don't have time for translation."

I played a bit of the tape for Rezvan, my friend from Iran. "It's not Arabic!" she declared, shaking her head. What could it be?

Rezvan and I tried several other students from other countries in the Arab world. No one recognized a single word.

Dejected, I drove home. There was not enough time to get another tape or letter. I cried. That's always my first step in time of trouble, but then, I quickly followed with step two. I joined my husband in front of the television.

He was watching *Petrocelli*, a detective of extraordinary abilities. The crime for that episode was solved when Petrocelli deduced that a tape had been taped over. He had a technician separate the two tapings and solved the mystery! Is God good?

By the next morning I had a dozen phone numbers for companies who specialized in electronics. I started calling early.

"I have a cassette tape I suspect is double-taped," I said, very authoritatively. "Can you separate the two?"

The answers were very much alike from 11 of the companies. Some of them thought I was a little weird; some of them thought I was a lot weird.

My last call was to Powell Electronics. I explained my problem to a young man named Greg. He thought a minute, then said, "I don't think that can be done."

"Petrocelli did it," I fired back.

"He did?" Greg asked. "Who is Petrocelli?"

It took a while to explain, but to my great joy, Greg said, "Well, I could give it a try."

"Way to go!" I blasted his ear drum. Then I asked cautiously, "How much?"

"If I do it, $10; if I don't, zero."

"You've got a deal! I'll be there with the tape in a jiffy," I answered.

He did it! Merrell had taped over an American Medical Association lecture tape on digitalis. The original had not erased. Greg separated the channels and saved my life.

That particular deadline on medical missions in the Middle East had another wild experience. Jim Young was my Yemen correspondent, and he had advised me to ask Dean Fitzgerald in Jordan to be my contact at the hospital in Ajloun, Jordan.

Then Jim chuckled, "You two should know each other! Dean's a card, but he's not much to write. I hear that he doesn't even write his mother!"

I accepted the challenge. I wrote Dean Fitzgerald, and I told him he was the only one I was writing in Jordan.

"If you don't write me, I won't write about Jordan and nobody will pray for you," I added.

Jim Young suspected that Dean would not write. He wrote a

lot about Jordan and sent it with his stuff on Yemen. Then I learned from the Foreign Mission Board that the Ajloun hospital might close soon.

I did not hear from Dean Fitzgerald. Finally, I put together the session with what I had, and met the deadline.

Thirty-five days after the deadline, a letter arrived from Dean Fitzgerald. It was a masterpiece.

I called Adrianne Bonham, the editor of *Royal Service*. "Do you want to write the part on Jordan over?" she asked.

"No, what I wrote is correct and what is needed, but can I do an article using Dean's letter?" I begged.

"Go ahead," she agreed, "and we'll see if it fits in."

So I wrote "Dear Mr. Missionary." (*Royal Service*, November 1976, pp. 2-3.) I recorded a few lines from Dean's letter and then I made a few comments. Here is a sample:

"I used to have big ideas about rocking the world toward God, but now it boils down to the fact that we are happy here. This seems to be the slot God has for us to fill. So here we are, filling it. We wouldn't trade living here for anywhere else.

"Did God "call" us here? I think so. The seven-league missionary boots we stepped into ten years ago have lost a lot of their gloss. They may look like ordinary shoes now, but they fit more comfortably.

"Dona and I are just doing a job that needs doing—like thousands of other Baptists who are at work in the states doing what God has for them to do. Not very inspirational, is it?"

Perhaps the most inspiring thing I've read in a hundred years. Please, God, help me fill my shoes here at home a whole lot better.

"Now for a hair-raising missionary story, lessee . . ."

In my defense I'd like to point out I have never in my whole life asked for a "hair-raising missionary story."

Of all the things I've ever written, that is still my favorite. I counted that assignment all joy!

Words have always captivated me,
the sounds,
the sights, the smells,
They transport me a world away,
to people I've never seen.

The stories spun by writers' pen,
their power,
their majesty,
I find myself in shadowed mosque,
I hear the calls to prayer.

Lord, take my words, my feeble words,
Please touch them,
Use them, Lord.
So hearts will burn with your great love
For your lost world
out there.

Proudly, I placed the copy in his hands and waited for his reply. "Do you mean to tell me it's just a paperback?" he said.

And the Lord's Finger Writ

I would meet my latest deadline and declare to all who would lend an ear that I'd never write again! Then a new contract would come in the mail, without any pressure at all, and I'd find myself signing away another year of peace and contentment.

A lot of factors played into my continuing to say yes. Ramona Wentworth's church opening its doors after that first migrant article was one. Another was the topics that came my way. I fell in love with Honduras, Costa Rica, and Guyana. And the Lord's finger writ on the manuscript paper: "Everybody ought to know in Honduras." I loved working with the Lord! Another reason I kept writing was that I always survived. I told myself that at the darkest moments.

In 1974 I accepted a really big assignment, the Week of Prayer for Foreign Missions. I had an idea that Editor Laurella Owens allowed me to explore. There was so much material to digest in the week of prayer programs, I felt they lost their punch.

"Would it be possible," I asked Laurella, "to feature just one missionary each day?" I promised that each of the five would be from a different part of the world. Each would be engaged in a different kind of work. My clincher argument was that the prayertime would be major, covering the area, not just the country, of the featured missionary. Laurella agreed to let me try.

Carefully and prayerfully, I chose the five missionaries: Gloria Thurman, Bangladesh; John David Hopper, Austria; Wana Ann Fort, Rhodesia; Julian King, Brazil; and Faye Pearson, Taiwan. Only one, Gloria Thurman, was a good friend. After writing the material, I claimed the other four as special friends also.

In 1976, I was asked to come to WMU, SBC, as an editor. I

was thrilled to the bottom of my soul and my soles. After talking and listening to the Lord, to my husband, and to others, I declined. In writing my letter to WMU I quoted one of my favorite authors, Louis Evely, a Catholic priest. In *That Man Is You*, Evely talks about the healing of the Gadarene demoniac. After being healed, the demoniac begged to go with Christ. He was sent home—to serve.

Evely's narrative continues with Jesus saying:
"Work for others;
   talk to them about Me,
   tell the world how merciful I am,
      instead of daydreaming about this boat
         that isn't meant for you.
And don't think of your life as a poor second choice:
   it's a beautiful life,
      and you can use it to satisfy all those people
         who need to have you show them
            'what the Lord's done'
            and what His love can accomplish."
What most of us lack is pride and joy:
         the thrilling awareness
         that we have a mission
         and that we're serving God
            wherever we are
            from morning to night."

I continued the letter, saying, "God has given me 'the thrilling awareness of my mission where I am.' It may not be much by the world's measure, but it's 'my mission' according to the Lord."

I've never regretted my decision. Well, maybe once—the big mix-up of 1977. For the first time in my writing career, I was allowed to chose my next assignment. I had loved doing the week of prayer so much that I chose to do the Week of Prayer for Foreign Missions for 1977. A close second was a whole issue devoted to Indonesia.

I completed the week of prayer material and prepared to have a nice long winter nap. Two restful months went by until the editorial assistant of *Royal Service* called asking if I needed any help on the Indonesia issue?

"What are you talking about?" I sputtered.

A change in editors had been accomplished with relative ease. Only one small casualty—my name had been penciled in for a whole issue on Indonesia. The material was due in little over a month! May 1978 *Royal Service* is a miracle. I didn't have the specifications for the magazine. When I got them I nearly fainted. I was responsible for *six* pieces of material. I needed help, fast.

I had recently read some excellent material written by Indonesian missionary William McElrath. Maybe if I could map out what I needed, he could help me.

Baptist Women's Meeting: Indonesian churches. I jotted down—city church and village church on Java, church on Sumatra. What does it look like, outside and inside. Who preaches? Describe. What do they sing? My list grew to ten questions.

"Dear Mr. McElrath," I wrote, "can you get three people to describe each of these churches? *Quickly?*"

Prayer Group: Medical Ministry in Indonesia.

"Mr. McElrath, can you find someone at Kediri and someone at Bukittinggi to tell me how the work is going in our hospitals? I need *lots* of prayer requests. *Quickly!*"

Current Missions Group: Theological Education by Extension

"Mr. McElrath, I need someone who teaches, someone who writes the material, and someone to tell about a student." "Oh, yes, *quickly!*"

Two special feature articles

"Mr. McElrath, would you ask Glenn Ingouf to share about the death of her daughter, Ann, if she can? And, would you write a special feature of your own choosing?"

Round Table Group: I didn't have to write Mr. McElrath about this. I only had to read three books and review them.

I filled two airforms and literally covered them with prayer all the way to Indonesia. God did more than His share. As the McElraths were pulling out of their driveway—going to mission meeting, where all the missionaries would be, they checked the mail. Both of my letters were there. At the mission meeting Mac read my letters. After each request he'd say, "Who will do a city church on Java?" Two insisted: Liz Corwin and Barbara Beevers. And so it went until every request was parceled out. "*Quickly!*" emphasized Mac, "and pray. Baptist Women will be studying and praying all of May. Who knows what God will do!"

Letters poured in. How could I give less than my best? I wrote night and day.

After a week the phone rang. "Barbara, I am Virginia Harper. My husband and I have just arrived on furlough. We are your contact for Kediri. The material is ready," she said. "Call us—it's not long distance—and we'll check everything."

I loved her immediately. "I've just completed the BW meeting on the churches . . ." I began.

"Oliver," she called, "get on the other phone!"

They checked every word I wrote. The Lord, the Harpers, the wonderful missionaries in Indonesia, and I made the deadline!

I had not completely recovered from Indonesia when Adrianne Bonham called me for a meeting. "Would you pray about writing one of the *Woman I Am* series—the one on decision making?" she asked.

I agreed to pray about it. I nearly worried the Lord to death about that book. I went down to the wire on this one—to the very day I had to give Adrianne an answer.

I told my dad about the book. I hadn't confided in him before, because he had been quite ill. Now he was improving physically, but deep depression had set in. His will to live was a matter of real concern.

"Daddy, I've been asked to write a book," I said.

Silence. Then, a twinkle came to his eyes and a smile (could it be?) touched his lips.

"I don't see why you shouldn't," he said.

"Thank you, Lord," I've prayed over and over since that day. I knew my dad wouldn't die until he saw that book his daughter was writing. God gave me a sign; he gave Daddy the will to live.

The follow-up to that incident was hilarious. I gave Daddy the first copy of *The Dynamic Woman I Am: Decision Making with God*. Proudly, I placed the copy in his hands and waited for his reply. "Do you mean to tell me it's just a paperback?" he said.

Yours for the Giving was my next big project. It was the emphasis book for WMU on spiritual gifts. I had superb editors on both of the books, Eljee Bentley on *Dynamic Woman* and Deena Newman on *Yours for the Giving*. I'm glad to say we came out on the other side better friends than before.

Now about this book, *Count It All Joy*. I found it difficult to believe anybody would be interested in my wild stories. I read a chapter to my husband early on. "Who in the world would be interested in that?" he asked. (Incidentally, it was the chapter on Homer and that June-girl. Well, I suspect old June-girl might be interested!) I haven't read anymore to him, but in my heart I think he could be right. I figure that the Lord and WMU are both taking a big chance on me—and have been for years.

Taking a Chance

Lord,
You really took a chance with Abraham.
He could have said,
"Forget it, Lord. Not my son!"
or
"Why me, Lord? Haven't I always tried to be
good?"
He could have refused to go
Or turned around half way there.
He could have bought a lamb on the way
Or found one in somebody's pasture.
He could have plunged the knife into his own
heart—
Easier than killing his son.
Yes, you do know about that, don't you?
Forgive me, Father.
You're taking a real chance on me, too.

Reprinted from *encounter!*
July-August-September 1982

"Daddy, I won't be afraid if you will hold my hand."

Soul Sister in Bangladesh

I know that I met Tom and Gloria Thurman during their first furlough home in 1969 because the first letters in my Bangladesh (then East Pakistan) file are dated that year. I haven't a clue as to when I first talked with them. It seems inconceivable that I failed to mark that day in red! I know they came to Columbiana to visit us before they left to go back to the field the last of June. Philip, their oldest son, took back some of Jackie and Jennifer's toys with him. Tom and Gloria took back our love and our promise to pray. We never suspected how stretched our prayer wings would become before next we saw each other.

Let me tell about my friend, Gloria Thurman.

"Oh, God, if you will cause her to live, she will be yours," Nancy Philpot prayed as she looked down at her tiny, premature baby. God heard that prayer offered in behalf of the baby born in 1941 in the little south Alabama town of McWilliams. He was to lay claim to that promise in a wonderful unfolding of His will. That baby was Gloria.

Gloria's family was Methodist, but when they moved to Camden, Alabama, when she was in the eighth grade, she accepted Christ as her Saviour at Enon Baptist Church. Two years later she committed her life to missions. At the same time, at New Orleans Baptist Theological Seminary, Tom Thurman surrendered his life to mission service. They had never met. It would be four years before that fateful meeting.

College seemed out of the question, but God opened the doors and Gloria entered Troy State College (now University). During her sophomore year God confirmed His call. Gloria was working with international students in the Baptist Student Union;

most of them were Muslim. She attended the international student retreat sponsored by Alabama's Woman's Missionary Union at Thanksgiving. As she shared what Jesus meant to her with students from all over the world, she realized God could use her on the foreign missions field. The call became real.

That same year, 1960, Gloria met Tom Thurman. God had been preparing both of them for His service and for each other. In 1962 they were married. They applied for appointment to East Pakistan.

Gloria remembers their first day in East Pakistan. They landed in Dhaka, the capital city, on December 7, 1965. The war between India and Pakistan had just ended. Soldiers surrounded the airport, which was in darkness. After a long hour, someone turned on the light.

"No one was there to meet us," Gloria recalls. "But a missionary from another board came in, spotted us, saw we were strangers and scared to death. He came to our rescue and called our mission. In that dark airport, in a strange new land, we knew calm assurance: This is the place we are to serve."

Language school occupied their first year. They studied the Bengali language and learned to live among the masses of people. Bangladesh is about the size of Arkansas but is home to over 115 million people.

After language school, the Thurmans moved to the city of Comilla where Tom did evangelistic work in the surrounding villages. Gloria began learning what a missionary homemaker is all about. "It means," says Gloria, "that I make the mayonnaise and the buttermilk and decide what to do with that piece of meat, whatever it is. The electricity is off. I get out the kerosene burner. It will be days before Tom will get home from preaching in the villages. And I'm sure that is a labor pain! Philip, our first child, was born during our first year in Comilla."

Gloria also discovered that she had a dazzling variety of other ministries:

Instant-vacancy-filler in the church. She had expected to work with children, but choir director or pianist?

Official hostess, tour guide, and innkeeper. The Thurmans have had meetings in the front yard, backyard, and living room, all at the same time. They have had 40 people to stay over. "It has not always been easy," Gloria says, "but I thank God for the opportunity of sharing our Christian home."

Relief distributor. The Thurmans don't have a lot to share, but the Bengalis have so little. They have seen Tom's pajamas appear at church as a sari blouse for a mother and pants for her son. Gloria's blouse becomes a Sunday dress for a little girl. A cabbage from their garden feeds a family without food for days.

Quack ministry. In a land of cholera, smallpox, malaria, and leprosy, Gloria can do no more than clean a sore, bandage a bleeding stump of a hand, give a fevered child an aspirin. But she does it with such love, praying that each patient will come to know a little of God's love.

After learning the ropes, it was furlough time. After furlough, the Thurmans went to the city of Faridpur. Four months later, their second son, David Olive, was born.

Then came the dark days of 1970. In a letter home, Tom explained the family crisis.

The doctor told us that the silver-dollar-sized ringworm-type growth on Gloria's left ankle is leprosy. The biopsy indicated tuberculoid leprosy. The report further states, however, that she is responding to the treatment of sulfone medication. It appeared for a while that we might have to return to the States for treatment. We were willing to go if necessary, but we had just come to feel at home here. We were meeting a real need; there had been a response to our witness. Ten years ago we made a decision to come; this year we had to make the same decision in reverse—to go if He willed. We carried this indecision for three months; one night about midnight, we took our heavy load to God. We prayed for His leadership. It did not matter if we went or stayed; we were ready to do His will. We feel confident about the treatment here, probably the best available in the world, for this is a country of 3 million lepers.

During this experience we came again to the challenge at the time of our appointment: "I will sing unto the Lord, because he hath dealt bountifully with me" (Psalm 13:6).

We sing best when we sing from the heart. Our wings of faith are stretched to soar into the darkness of the unknown. But His everlasting arms are present to hold us up.

God did hold the Thurmans up. They stayed. Gloria took a complete test when they returned home on furlough in 1973, and she was given a clean bill of health.

But 1970 continued to be a year of terror. November 13, 1970—the long, dark night of suffering already termed the worse natural disaster of the twentieth century—left half a million Bengalis dead. Huge waves, swept by typhoon winds, brought death and destruction to a degree previously unknown to man.

Pure drinking water was an immediate necessity. The mission

decided to sink tube wells in 200 villages. Jim McKinley, R. T. Buckley, Don Jones, Carl Ryther, and Tom Thurman walked many miles carrying pipes and pumps to remote areas where no vehicle could go. They ate (and sometimes fasted) and slept in the villages. They worked long hours with the smell of death in their nostrils.

The need was so desperate, they worked man-killing hours under the broiling sun. Each day began at 3:30 A.M. At every site they encountered parents wailing for lost children.

Only a few months passed before the nightmare of war grabbed the suffering country. February and March 1971 were uneasy with civil unrest. Trouble had been brewing between East and West Pakistan for some time. War broke out in March. Heavy fighting took place in Dhaka and followed in other major towns. Word came that all foreigners were being evacuated. The Carl Ryther family and the Thurman family stayed in Faridpur, which was relatively quiet.

When the army arrived in April, mortar fire fell on the mission workshop. The Thurmans lay on the bedroom floor for protection from stray bullets.

The last three months of the war were the most dangerous times. The Thurmans and the Jim McKinley family survived it together in the mission guest house in Dhaka. On more than one occasion they huddled together in the narrow hallway, seeking safety.

To assure their families during the anxious days, Gloria wrote home: "In all that has happened, God has been very real. He has protected us from harm and given His peace in troubled times. He has taught a clearer meaning of bearing the burdens of one another. We believe that after great suffering God is able to do great things. The people continue to come and we continue to listen. If they find something of God's love, then our staying will not be in vain."

One night before the war's end, the Thurmans were stumbling along in the darkness during a night bombing, finding their way to safety. Philip, the oldest son, said, "Daddy, I won't be afraid if you will hold my hand." Tom and Gloria prayed that same prayer that night.

December 16, 1971—day of victory! A new nation was born. God allowed the Thurmans to be a part of it.

The land, however, was devastated. Thousands of refugees returning from India were homeless. It seemed that all of Bangladesh was hungry. One village had survived on water hyacinths for over a month.

The Thurmans shared all they had with the suffering Bengalis. They helped in the massive relief efforts undertaken by many groups. The Baptist mission built simple houses, costing about $200 each. Three thousand houses were built in a short time. Inadequate by American standards, to families exposed to monsoon rains, these simple houses were palaces.

Gloria said of those days, "We thank God for the privilege of serving during the hard times. We experienced His amazing grace over and over again."

I saw the McKinleys of Bangladesh before I did the Thurmans after these difficult days. In fact, I accosted Jim McKinley as he arrived at Glorieta in 1973. "Is Gloria really all right?" I asked.

"Completely," he assured me. "Just a little scar, no bigger than a half dollar remains. She's fine!"

I could hardly wait for the Thurmans to arrive on furlough. Gloria and I cried buckets of tears (she calls us the weeping prophetesses) and hugged again and again before we could talk.

"I am so mad at the Lord," I fumed.

"Oh, Barbara, everything about the leprosy was so good," Gloria declared. She recounted to me all the miracles: a World Health Organization doctor in Dhaka who diagnosed tuberculoid leprosy which is not contagious, good medical help readily available in Bangladesh. "Best of all," she said, "the people were so touched that I had 'their' disease and chose to stay. The Lord used the leprosy to soften hearts. We saw response almost immediately."

During that furlough, Gloria told the Woman's Missionary Union staff at their headquarter's building in Birmingham that we were soul sisters. I remember the absolute jolt of unworthiness that I felt. Gloria is the soul. I am the sister. I was honored and I treasure that title very much.

The Thurmans went back to crisis, again. Flooding is a constant threat in Bangladesh. A month after arrival from furlough, the water was three-feet deep in the compound at Faridpur. In 1975 the country had a coup and later, a counter-coup. But during dangerous days, God protected the Thurmans.

In the fall of 1976, the senior high Acteens at First Baptist, Columbiana, took on the Thurmans as a special project. We deposited more than $500 in the Thurman bank account. We could not believe what that money provided:

1. A yoke of oxen for plowing for a village
2. A yoke of oxen with a wagon and mustard seed oil crushing machine for another village
3. Medicine to supply a clinic

4. Purchase of land for a widow
5. A rice husking machine for another widow
6. Purchase of land and fish nets for another village

After their 1979 furlough, the Thurmans returned to a different locale—Gopalganj, a river town about 60 miles south of Faridpur. It took 12 hours to reach Dhaka although it was only 100 miles away! Philip, age 12, left for boarding school in India. I wept with Tom and Gloria.

It seems there was never a let up. In 1988 the worst flood in 40 years struck the country. Two-thirds of Bangladesh was under water. Millions of people were left homeless. Farms and businesses were ruined. Southern Baptist disaster and hunger funds provided food, new crops, tube wells, animal vaccine, and ducks for meat and eggs. By 1990 more than 1,300 tube wells had been provided for clean drinking water.

In the midst of more suffering, God blessed. In Gopalganj in 1988, 306 had been baptized. The missionaries had prayed for three new churches in the area; God had given ten!

Before going back from furlough in 1989, Tom set an important goal for himself. He was determined to be the first missionary to sleep in the "missionary" room in our new home! More specifically, he wanted to beat Jerry Bedsole! Actually, home missionaries and dear friends, C. J. and Barbara Langton from North Mankato, Minnesota, beat both of them to the draw. They stayed with us only a month or so after we moved. But Tom beat Jerry, and was proud of it. I expect a plaque from Bangladesh any day!

Tom and Gloria made a hurried trip back to the US the last of July 1990. Son Philip had claimed a beautiful bride, Lori. Homer and I traveled to Jackson, Mississippi, on a sweltering August 4 to witness the vows.

A remarkable thing occurred at the wedding. I was committed to writing this book, but I had not yet decided on a title. In the hush and candlelight of that beautiful sanctuary, the title came: *Count It All Joy.* It had been the theme of Tom and Gloria's life. I, too, had learned to thank God for the shadows and storms. That was it! I rumbled around in my noisy purse, searching for a scrap of paper and a pen. After several sharp looks from my dignified husband, I found pen and paper and recorded the words.

So, Soul Sister, I owe my title to you, and so much more.

She has seen the star
And traveled to the East.
A journey of love
for God.
A journey of love
for Bangladesh,
for surely that star shone also
for the Bengali people.

She has seen His cross.
And that cross, that sacrifice
overshadowed loneliness,
tidal wave, monsoon,
war's crippling fear, and
the dread scourge of leprosy.

Grace so amazing—to be able to see.
Love so divine—to be able to understand.
She has seen His star!
Oh, God grant us
eyes that see,
hearts that love.
We, too, would see your star
and follow you.

*I'd said all along that two things would bring him
through, his strong faith in God and his sense of
humor.*

Room for Two in Solitary

In 1972 the Vietnam war held us all captive. Many had family fighting in that jungle conflict. All of us had friends. Columbiana's heart had been broken over the death of Sergeant First Class Melvin Gunter. Melvin and his wife, Myra, were members of First Baptist Church.

Then, on June 27, 1972, the plane of First Lieutenant Richard H. McDow was shot down over North Vietnam. The official letter to Rick's family, dated July 1, said this:

"On the morning of 27 June 1972, Rick departed Takhli Royal Thai Air Force Base with his aircraft commander, Major Robert C. Miller, for an escort mission over North Vietnam. Rick's job was to escort other F-4 Phantoms which were dropping chaff in the area prior to the strike force entering the target area. After egressing the area, Rick's four ship flight was refueled inflight and returned to an area southwest of Hanoi where one of the strike F-4s had gone down. Their job was to assist in locating the aircrew visually or by radio so Search and Rescue aircraft could pick them up. After one unsuccessful attempt, they refueled and returned for another try. Again unsuccessful, they were departing the area when Rick's flight was vectored toward MIGs which were a threat to the Search and Rescue effort. While attempting visual contact with the MIGs, Rick's airplane and the one on his right wing were attacked from behind by enemy aircraft which came in at low level and high speed. Both airplanes were hit by heat seeking missiles fired from the MIGs. Both F-4s were observed going down and all other crewmembers observed four good parachutes. The other two F-4s in Rick's flight remained in the area and watched them descend to mark their locations and to protect them. The two F-4s departed later for fuel and returned immediately to await the arrival of rescue aircraft. When the rescue aircraft arrived they had voice contact with Rick and he reported that he was on the ground safely and was uninjured. Two of the other crewmembers including Major Miller were rescued that day, but the rescue helicopter was hit by heavy ground fire and had to withdraw because of damage and approaching darkness. The area that they went down in is sparsely populated, mountainous, and densely foliated. Unfortunately, Rick landed on the hillside toward a valley and village. Since enemy forces were present in the area, Rick's capture is a possibility. We all feel he is in good condition, however, and the electronic search is continuing in hopes that he and the other crewmember, Captain Tom Hanton, are moving to a safer place to attempt radio contact.

"There is no way to express the sorrow we all feel. We are all doing all that can be done and we are praying for all that is beyond our power."

We were devastated. The whole town prayed "for all that was beyond our power."

The McDow family was an integral part of our town. James T. McDow, Sr., Jimmy, was a deacon at First Baptist. He had served as chairman of the deacons several times, as Sunday School director and teacher, as moderator of Shelby Baptist Association. A successful businessman, Jimmy owned and managed McDow Motor Company, a Chevrolet dealership. He had just completed a term as an Alabama state senator.

Jimmy's wife, Miki, had died of cancer three years earlier. She, too, had been a leader in the church and community. There were three McDow children. The oldest son, Jim, had been one of my star debaters. Rick was serving in the air force after graduating from the University of Alabama. Patti had just completed her junior year at Shelby County High School.

Jimmy had married Marion Blackerby after Miki's death. She and her daughter, Kathy, were part of the family now.

When the call came informing the McDows that Rick was missing, six of us were scheduled to leave in three days to travel to Glorieta Baptist Conference Center in New Mexico for the first National Acteens Conference. I was leading conferences. Patti McDow, Kathy Blackerby, Vicki Joiner, Peggy Armstrong, and Sherri Hughes were accompanying me. They were scheduled to be in the opening procession in costumes representing the major areas of the world. Each was to carry a flag from her country. Except for Patti; she was to dress like a typical teenager (that meant a miniskirt in 1972) and carry the brand new, first-time-shown Acteens flag. The last person in the opening procession was to be Janet Lynn, Olympic ice skating gold medalist. She was to carry the Olympic flag.

The girls were also scheduled to speak on program about the Ethiopian mission action project we had done the year before.

The call to the McDows came in the middle of the night. They, in turn, called our house and we went to their home immediately. A whole lot of praying started in the den of the McDow home and spread all over the town, the country, and even to Ethiopia.

No fresh news followed the communique. In fact, it was two months before word came that Rick had been captured and was being held as a prisoner of war at the Hanoi Hilton.

The decision was made for us to go on to NAC. It was a long trip under good circumstances, but with our concern about Rick, it was a difficult three-day drive. God took care of us, and when we got to Glorieta, He gave us thousands of additional prayer warriors. They prayed for Rick then, but they also prayed for the long haul. Many wore POW bracelets with Rick's name on them.

Months later Christine Griffin, an Acteens leader from Lumberton, North Carolina, wrote, "Today I was watching the television when they showed some of the returning prisoners of war. When they announced First Lieutenant Richard H. McDow and I saw him walk through the door of the plane, I just fell on my knees in front of the television and thanked God for sending him home!"

There were many anxious days before we saw Rick walk off that plane. We thanked God when word came that he was captured. Beverly, Rick's wife, immediately started packing boxes to send to him. She majored on Cracker Jacks.

"Cracker Jacks?" I asked. "Why in the world? They are sure to get stale and they take up a lot of room."

"Rick likes Cracker Jacks," she explained.

Little did Beverly know the joy that Rick got from those Cracker Jacks. His packages were carefully examined. Right in front of him, a guard opened a pack of Cracker Jacks with those funny little prizes. When the guard found the little prize in one package, he shouted, "Ah, ha!" He slammed it against the wall with his palm, then threw it to the floor and repeatedly jumped and stomped on it. He thought it was a sophisticated device sent to his prisoner. Rick loved it!

To keep busy, Beverly accompanied me when I went somewhere to speak. She was my navigator. Her father, Jack Upchurch, thought that was hilarious. He and Homer both feared we'd end up who-knows-where. I tried to explain that a lot of places I go are to who-knows-where and turn right.

We always found our place. Then I'd divide my time with Beverly and we'd leave a whole church or association praying for Rick's safe return.

Sure enough, nine months and one day after his capture, Rick was released. What glorious news! At least half of Columbiana met his flight when he arrived at Maxwell Air Force Base in Montgomery. Homer and I had the joy of having dinner with the McDow family at the Officer's Club. Rick looked wonderful. The only thing the doctors could find wrong with him was one cavity. I'd said all along that two things would bring him through, his strong faith in God and his sense of humor. He shared some of both with us that night. He told about the Cracker Jacks and he told about solitary.

"Solitary is a small dark hole," he explained. "You must bend double to fit in. Then they close down the door. The pain becomes excruciating and the loneliness can drive a man mad. What the Viet Cong didn't know, however, was that my solitary had room enough for two. God was there with me every moment of the time."

Rick needed that strong faith then and when he got home. On June 27, 1973, exactly one year after his plane was shot down, cancer claimed the life of his father, Jimmy.

Cancer continued to strike the McDow family. Patti's young preacher husband, Joe O'Quinn, only 34, died of leukemia in December 1989.

But there has also been great joy. Rick and Beverly have two wonderful daughters, Kelly and Lisa. In July 1989, Kelly attended the fifth National Acteens Conference in San Antonio, Texas. On commitment night, I served as a counselor. Someone said to me, "There is a girl outside who wants to see no one but you." It was Kelly. At the first National Acteens Conference we had prayed her daddy home. Now, 17 years later, at the fifth conference Kelly told the Lord she'd go anywhere He called her—even Southeast Asia!

Dear Kelly, it could be that God will call you to Southeast Asia or perhaps to the Middle East. You see, right now Lieutenant Colonel Richard H. McDow and his entire squadron are stationed in Saudi Arabia. I'm so glad that God is stationed there, too.

God,
Are you there? It's so dark in here.
What was that?
Are they coming with water?
I'm so thirsty, Lord.

No,
The footsteps are fading—
They're not coming with water for me.
What's that scrabbling?
Not rats . . . I hate rats.

God,
I'm so hungry. Will I eat at all today?
Garbage, it's garbage.
But I must stay alive.
I must stay alive . . .

Lord,
I know you're here with me.
You don't have to be.
But you hung on that cross for me,
And you promised to be with me always.
Even in solitary.

Thank you, Jesus.

P.S. On Thursday, February 28, 1991, Iraq conceded defeat. Operation
Desert Storm ended with a cease-fire and a complete allied victory
after a five-and-a-half week air assault followed by a four-day ground
offensive.

On Thursday, March 21, the 354th Technical Fighter Wing returned
to their home base in South Carolina. Lieutenant Colonel Richard H.
McDow, the commander, was the lead pilot. Rick had come home
again.

"Pray about it," she urged.
"No! God might tell me to do it!" I replied.

The Chicago Nine

In the fall of 1976, I was invited to speak at the Illinois Acteens Convention. Evelyn Tully, the Woman's Missionary Union associate asked me, very specifically, to speak the first session on migrants. It was written in big, bold letters in the colorful program: MIGRANTS.

I love to talk about our migrant work. When I do, anybody within hearing distance takes for granted that I really love them. Migrants are the bottom of the totem pole when ranked with any minority group. Therefore, if I love migrants (and I do) then I must *really* love any other minority group (and I do).

That first night I intended to talk about migrants; I had prepared to talk about migrants. But I didn't. I don't know why; I just didn't!

At two o'clock in the morning, there arose a great disturbance outside my window. Curious, I peeped out to see what was happening. Two vans had arrived. On the side was painted Rockwell Baptist Chapel, Chicago, Illinois. Girls were piling out: red and yellow, black and white. They looked like a mini-United Nations. God had stopped my tongue! He knew I needed to wait for Rockwell to arrive to share about migrants.

The next morning I talked about migrants even though the program now said something completely different. I cannot believe that Evelyn Tully keeps asking me to come back!

After I finished, the Rockwell Acteens came up to the front and sort of stood around. Their faces said, "You really like us!" And I did. What they actually said was, "Want to go to McDonald's with us for lunch?

"Why not?" I responded, hugging them all.

That night at the banquet, they saved a place for me at their table. Then they came by to pick me up to go to breakfast—at McDonald's, of course.

Marilee Shockey, home missionary at Rockwell, said, "The girls really love you." My reply was that the girls loved me because I loved them.

"Guess how many are Christians?" Before I could guess, she continued, "Two—my daughters, Jeanne and Julie. It's so hard for the girls to accept the Lord. It means breaking with family and culture, but they are listening and learning."

I saw a light bulb go on in her mind. "You know what you need to do, Barbara? You need to bring a group of young people to work at Rockwell this summer!"

"No way, Marilee!" I said, "Our kids are small-town kids. Me, too. We can't do that. We don't have the money anyway."

"Pray about it," she urged.

"No! God might tell me to do it!" I replied.

And I did *not* pray about it. I didn't tell anybody about the invitation, but God bugged me constantly. I'd open a *National Geographic* and the whole issue would be on Chicago. I'd go to the airport and every other travel poster would say "Visit Chicago." I'd turn on the television and Chicago would be in the news. "Gang members picked up a police car today and dumped it into Lake Michigan."

"See!" I'd storm at the Lord, "It's not a safe place to go!"

My resistance wore down. One day I walked into the office of my pastor, Charles Stroud.

"I've got to talk to you," I said. "We have been invited to bring a SMAY team to Chicago. SMAY was Summer Mission Activities for Youth, coed, and a forerunner of Acteens Activators.

Charles said, "I'd go." Charles Stroud is about 6-feet-2-inches tall and has big, broad shoulders. If you're planning to go to a ghetto, Charles Stroud is a good man to go with!

"How many do they want on the team?" he asked.

"Nine or ten," I replied.

"Well, John can go," he wrote down the name of his big football playing son.

"Sure can," I agreed.

"And Danny King," he jotted down another varsity player. I nodded affirmatively.

"Jackie," he said.

"Not my Jackie; she's too pretty." He ignored me and kept writing.

"Connie Brown," he wrote.

"She's too blonde," I cautioned.

"Denise Bean, Nancy Isbell, and Mary Norton," he stated positively. He named another outstanding Acteen and two wonderful Acteens leaders. "With you, that's nine."

He was right. It was nine and all were top-notch.

"But we don't have a van," I pointed out, "We don't even have a drop in the van fund. And nobody will lend us a van to take to Chicago to get ripped off!"

"A van," he wrote down on his list. "And we need a cheap place to stay and a cheap place to eat."

"They probably don't have a Day's Inn and McDonald's probably doesn't go that far north," I reminded him.

Charles added those to his list. "Now let's pray," he said.

"I was afraid you were going to say that," I moaned. We prayed and I knew we were on our way to the Windy City!

That night, I told Homer about Chicago. He looked at me with that look that says, "I have married a crazy woman!" However, the next morning he said, "Get ready. We need to go to Birmingham and trade in the station wagon. You have worn it out going to migrant camp." So we went to Birmingham and traded for a brand new red-and-white Volkswagen van which we named Jehosaphat, for he was a goodly king.

I wrote Marilee and told her we had a van. "Is there a cheap place to stay and a cheap place to eat?"

She wrote back, "Bring your bedrolls. You can sleep at Rockwell Chapel." I'll never forget that my bedroll was right in front of the Lord's Supper table. John Stroud remarked, "Barb, this time you really have put it all on the altar!"

One more problem arose. I was to be at Acteens Camp in Illinois at Lake Sallateeska, the week before going to Chicago. Homer insisted I take Jackie with me because she had a boyfriend on the front steps and one on the back steps. I called Evelyn Tully in Illinois; "Bring Jackie,too," she said. Homer broke the news to Jackie, who hated all camps. "No, *please*, no!" Jackie pleaded.

"You choose," Homer said, "camp or the nunnery." Reluctantly, Jackie went to Sallateeska, the most primitive of all WMU camps. She fell in love with it and with the counselors, especially Melanie Smith. Amazingly, the next two years she returned to Sallateeska as a counselor and loved every minute of it. In fact, when Jackie was chosen as a National Acteens Panelist in 1979, two states claimed her: Alabama and Illinois!

Jackie and I flew into Chicago from Sallateeska. The rest of the team left after church Sunday morning, June 26, 1977, and drove straight through. There was no money for motels. They arrived in Chicago during rush hour on Monday morning on an eight-lane freeway. That kept everybody's eyes open.

They followed directions carefully and finally reached Rockwell Baptist chapel. Around the chapel the early morning sun revealed once proud buildings falling into ruin. Burned-out buildings were ugly blots against the sky. Graffiti marked gang boundaries. Our ears were assaulted with sirens and horns from what had to be a million cars and motorcycles. We recognized lilting Spanish voices announcing the Puerto Rican nature of the neighborhood. Island blacks, American blacks, and a liberal sprinkling of eastern Europeans make the area multiracial and multilingual.

Rockwell Chapel stands in the middle of it all. In the heart of the city, Rockwell offers the answer, Jesus Christ.

We unloaded and unpacked. Schedules were worked out. We were to work in day care every morning from 8:00 to 10:00. At 10:30 we had three Big A Clubs. In the afternoon, four additional Big A Clubs. Special activities were planned for each night. We arrived back at Rockwell every night after midnight and had to prepare for the next day!

We knew the Bible clubs could locate prospects who could become involved in the Chapel and then come to know the Lord. We prayed that the mission action material, the Big A Club, would work in the inner city.

By the end of the first day, nearly 200 children had sung "You must love the Lord your God with all your heart." We had sung in the backyard at Mrs. Yulfo's apartment. We had sung on the Ortiz steps just inches from a busy highway. We had sung inside and outside all sorts of buildings.

Hundreds of puzzles had been worked; dozens of name tags identified Big A Club members. Our hands ached from Big A handshakes. We played Big A games with kids of every color and shape. Stories were told and retold. Bibles were given to stunned young people.

"You mean I can keep this for my own?"

When assured the Bible was truly his to keep, the 13-year-old's eyes widened in disbelief. Only after seeing his name on the flyleaf did he believe. We prayed that he would come to believe in the Man of the Book as well.

Columbiana teenagers had the privilege of working side by side with some of the finest people in the world. Floyd and Marilee Shockey are top-notch missionaries. We fell in love with the Shockey kids. By the end of the week we didn't even scream when Jim Shockey wove through the streets in the van! The Rockwell Acteens became sisters. We saw Chicago with this crew. They took us by boat, by el, by city bus, and by van all over Chicago. We saw the city's beauty as well as her decay. We visited the Baptist missions all over the city and even heard the glorious Rumanian choir sing. We ate the fabulous Spanish cooking of the Baptist Women at Rockwell. We ate Chinese and we ate the best pizza in the world at Pizza Deu.

The week ended too soon. Friday night a big rally was to close it out. Tickets had been printed to be distributed: "Admit one to Rockwell. Free movie: *Gospel Road* starring Johnny Cash. Special music. Special guests."

We walked the streets handing out stacks of tickets. The crowd started gathering before dark. We sang together, prayed together, and saw the story of Christ presented.

Then it was midnight. The van was loaded and the last good-byes said. We were on our way home, but not completely so. Chicago will always be a part of the Chicago Nine. And best of all, one of the nine felt God's call to return. Today Denise Bean is part of God's work force in Illinois.

Before the Shockeys left Chicago, Marilee wrote the history of the amazing Rockwell Chapel. She wrote me to say, "The Chicago Nine is now officially a part of history."

"I didn't believe you guys would come all the way from Alabama," one teenager said.

"Do you know how much I love you, Sandra?" I asked.

"Yes," she replied immediately.

"God loves you so much more. It's because we want you to know how much He loves you that we came."

I count Chicago all joy. I could have lived without the two-second cold showers . . . but that's another whole story!

Lakeshore Drive is a feast for the eyes,
It's beauty is an artist's delight.
The waves lap gently against the sand,
Clouds scudder 'cross the bluest of skies.

Humboldt is littered with foulest of trash,
The smells assault like a blow.
Garbage is left to fester like a sore,
And the children are discarded like junk.

Oh, Lord,
How can a city with beauty to spare,
Turn its eyes from the children out there?
So beautiful,
So gifted,
Don't let them be thrown away.
Save the children, Oh, Father,
Save the little child.

Oh, no! Isn't a week enough?
You want a life. . .

Anybody got a life to give
to Chicago?
Please. . .

Over 60 cans were filled with nearly 2,000 cookies and bars. My station wagon runneth over with Acteens, cookies, and Bibles.

Cookie Crumble and Other Assorted Crumbs

It all started with a tiny article on the back page of the newspaper. A Nigerian student, returning to his native country after completing two degrees in business administration, was met at the airport in Lagos and interviewed.

"Must be destined for an important government job or the son of an official," I thought.

"What did you think of America?" they asked him.

"Beautiful," he said.

"What about the educational system? Did you get a good education?" continued the newsman.

"Excellent," the young man replied. "I received a very good education."

"What do you think of the American home and their churches?" quizzed the reporter.

"I can't answer those questions," the student sadly observed. "I was never invited to either."

Those words pierced my heart! I could see one of our Southern Baptist missionaries approaching this young man. "Let me tell you about Jesus Christ. I've been sent by Christians in America to share with you about God who loves you."

If I were that young man I would reply, "That's funny. They didn't tell me about their God when I was living in America for six years."

"Somebody ought to do something!" I said. But I didn't mean me. I work with Acteens, and Acteens are not capable of working with international students.

Less than a month later a phone call changed my life and the lives of many Acteens. Bob Ford, the campus minister at the

University of Montevallo, less than 20 miles from Columbiana, called to ask for help. Two Chinese students from Malaysia had arrived on campus without bed linens. The students expected the University to furnish them.

"Could your Acteens help?"

We could. That very night we went over to the college loaded with sheets, pillows, towels, blankets, the works. I remember, in particular, the generosity of Jackie. We had everything we needed when the girls arrived at my house except bedspreads. Jackie went immediately and pulled the spreads from the twin beds in her room. I was not fooled. She had been begging for new spreads for some time!

At Montevallo, we met Daniel Loh, a product of our Southern Baptist missions work, whose father is a Baptist preacher in Malaysia. In fact, pastor Loh was called the Billy Graham of Malaysia. In addition, we met his friend, Seng Moon Cheng, also a Baptist and a first-year student at the University.

We all became friends. In the days that followed, Daniel and Moon visited our church and our home many times.

When dead week, the week before semester exams, arrived, we made another move. We knew many students received "care" packages from home with all kinds of goodies to enjoy while studying for exams. But not Daniel and Moon. Their mothers were halfway around the world. We decided we would provide snacks for them and other foreign students at the University. It was the beginning of Cookie Crumble.

That first year, 1975, we did everything wrong. We prepared for 12 students and there were nearly six times as many! Everywhere we went to deliver cookies, we found students we had not prepared for! We retreated to the station wagon and cried for the harm we had done. One Acteen declared that we had set back international diplomacy 20 years! I was in favor of forgetting the whole sorry mess. The Acteens, however, were bloody but unbowed. They decided that we should learn to do it right. They started making plans immediately.

The next year we started Cookie Crumble in October. We asked for and got a complete listing of all foreign students. Then we discovered what a big job we had ahead of us. There were 62 students from 20 different countries.

We gathered two-pound coffee cans and cookie tins and decoupaged them with Christmas paper. We made personal Christmas cards for all the students. And we started baking.

In October, we baked hundreds of brownies and wrapped them individually and froze them. In November, we baked

Congo bars, butterscotch bars, and coconut bars and froze them. In December, we began baking Christmas cookies of all kinds. We were sure that the students would know that First Baptist Columbiana Acteens loved them.

Then one of the Acteens said, "But how will they know that God loves them?" His Word. Of course, that was the answer. If only we could find Bibles or gospel portions in the language of each student. But where?

The American Bible Society! I had gone for a conference at the American Bible Society the spring before. I didn't have time to go, but I made the time. The trip had been a joy. I had gotten to know many wonderful Christians from many denominations from all over the United States. In particular, I had come to love Alice Ball, then vice president of the American Bible Society.

I called Alice, list in hand, and ordered Bibles. Soon boxes started arriving with Bibles in Yoruba and Hausa, Japanese and Chinese, Amharic and Swahili, Hindi and Bengali. Each was opened by the Acteens with great excitement. "You read this one starting at the back," exclaimed Kathy. "Denise, read this verse. It's John 3:16!" "Look at the beautiful Thai Bibles with gold lily pads on the front!"

Finally, the big day arrived. Over 60 cans were filled with nearly 2,000 cookies and bars. My station wagon runneth over with Acteens, cookies, and Bibles.

Daniel and Moon met us on campus, escorted us in and out of dorms, and carried boxes. All the work was worthwhile when we delivered the first can of cookies and the first Bible. Ahmed opened the door and saw a hall full of smiling teenaged girls. "We're Christians from the First Baptist Church of Columbiana," explained Deborah. "We've brought you some homemade cookies and brownies to eat while you're studying for finals," chimed in Connie. Then Jackie handed the student from Bangladesh a beautiful brown Bengali Bible. Ahmed opened the Bible, his eyes widened, and then he clutched it to his chest.

"It's the first thing I've seen in my language since I've been in America! Thank you, thank you."

As we left Ahmed's room, Moon said, "Ahmed is a Muslim, but he'll read that Bible because it's in his own language."

Christmas 1976 will long be remembered by Columbiana Acteens. Almost 2,000 years earlier, on the other side of the world, a baby was born in a manger—God's indescribable gift to the world. That Christmas, our Acteens shared the good news in many languages with students from all over God's world.

Michiko, a Japanese student, wrote, "The homemade cookies

are delicious. But particularly, I am enjoying reading the Japanese Bible."

Since that Christmas we have baked millions more cookies, wrapped a thousand or more cans, delivered box after box of Bibles. One Acteen said, "God may call some of us to go across the seas someday, but for now He has brought the world to us."

By 1986 we thought we had Cookie Crumble running like a finely-tuned machine. Then Krishna happened. By the eighties, it seemed all of Malaysia had discovered the University of Montevallo. Over 50 international students called Kuala Lumpur, Ipoh, Penang, even Borneo home. One Malaysian student from the capital city of Kuala Lumpur had a different sounding name: Krishna Papaniakam. The other Malaysians were Li's or Loh's or Cheng's, very Chinese.

"Krishna must be from India," I decided. "Many of the businessmen in Malaysia are from India." I had learned that fact in mission study.

We did not have an address for Krishna, only a post office box number. No matter, I would find out where he lived from one of the other Malaysian students.

We arrived at the University with 81 cans of cookies. We went back to Columbiana with one can of cookies still undelivered, the one for Krishna Papaniakam. We asked every Malaysian student of his whereabouts, no one had ever seen him. There were three students from India. None of them knew Krishna. Did he actually exist? Even the faculty liaison for the internationals had never seen Krishna.

Two days later the *Shelby County Reporter* ran a front page article on international students. We read the article because one of our favorite Malaysian students, Aileen, was pictured. Another student from Malaysia, without photo, was also featured: Krishna Papaniakam! Both were asked about their Christmas plans. Aileen described the wonderful holidays she had spent in the homes of American friends. She even mentioned Cookie Crumble. Krishna, on the other hand, described his first Christmas in America quite differently. He had spent the whole day at the Omelet Shoppe! My heart ached. And he didn't even have any cookies!

When the Acteens arrived that night for our Christmas meeting, many had the newspaper. "What are we going to do about Krishna?" they quizzed me.

"You will find Krishna, won't you, Barbara?" Mary Elizabeth pled. "Promise me you will find him, and ask him to come spend Christmas with you!"

103

"But I have no idea *how* to find him; we've already searched all of Montevallo for him," I reminded her.

"Call the paper," Lassie advised. "They found him."

I had to admit it was a good idea. I called the next morning. The article had been written by a University student. When I called the school, I discovered the student had finished exams and had gone home to Georgia for the holidays. No, they didn't know his phone number. Computers were already closed down (also home for the holidays, I supposed). Dead end!

What to do? I made ten posters. All said "KRISHNA PAPANI-AKAM! Call Barbara Joiner—669-6982. We want you to spend Christmas day with our family." I took the posters to Montevallo. I hit every fast-food place, including the Omelet Shoppe. I also left one taped to the post office door. Then I went home to wait for Krishna's call.

On Christmas Eve, I wrapped presents with a heavy heart. I had not heard from Krishna. It was past midnight when the phone rang. When I answered a voice said, "Mrs. Joiner?"

"Krishna, is this you?" He assured me that it was indeed.

"Do you mean what you say on the poster? Do you really want me to spend Christmas with your family?" he asked.

"Oh, Krishna," I responded, "my Christmas would be ruined if you didn't come!"

Early Christmas morning, before breakfast, Krishna arrived. We had a wonderful day together. Krishna was a delightful guest. When he left that night, he promised to come again. He did and we came to love him. We also knew exactly where he lived from that point until his graduation.

The second Christmas Krishna spent with us, he brought an ornament for our Christmas tree. He was fascinated by our tree. I am looking at that ornament as I write this shortly before Christmas. It has an honored place on our tree. Krishna's ornament is a beautifully crafted sitar, a stringed instrument of India.

Everytime I look at the sitar I am reminded that for many, there is still no room in the inn.

No room in the inn.
We sigh with grief
As we read the words.
No room for the Christ Child?
Selfish old innkeeper!
Didn't he know the Saviour had come?

But in dark city streets,
In heatless cramped rooms,
Little children shiver
Wrapped in rags.
No room for the child?
Selfish old world!
Don't they know the Saviour has come?

In small village towns,
Tables are empty.
Hungry stomachs face
Another long day.
No room for the child?
Selfish old Christian!
Don't you know the Saviour has come?

Every little child,
Every desperate mother,
Caught in the hopeless
Tangle of life.
No room for the child?
God forgive us all!
We don't recognize the Saviour when He comes.

I sat there in the spacious front seat and went over the whole sorry mess again, blaming God for everything.

You Can't Outgive God

I had started with mission studies, but then I found myself speaking and teaching everywhere. I could hardly believe that people in New York or Texas or California could understand me, much less like me and what I had to say.

God handled things nicely. Even though I didn't know when I needed to be at home, He always did. I never had to catch a plane when one of my children had a fever. I did not miss special parties or piano or dance recitals. I didn't even miss PTA meetings. (I could have missed a few of those!)

This went on for years; then the bottom fell out!

I had promised to go to Miami in February 1980 for a prayer retreat. It had been on my calendar well over a year. In December 1979, Jackie came home from her piano lesson at Samford University. She was enrolled in the University's fine piano preparatory program. They considered her a very talented, promising student. (Homer and I knew she was the most gifted student they had ever had.)

Jackie had decided to try for a piano scholarship. "I have three *long* classical pieces that I must memorize. Then I have to sight-read whatever the judges put before me. The third thing I have to do is a theory test that is supposed to be very hard."

"Anyway," she continued, "you have to go with me to Samford that day, February 13th, mark it on your calendar! You have to pray me through!"

My heart sank. I never remember what's on my calendar, but I knew that date, it was the Miami prayer retreat. Jackie was so excited that I didn't have the heart to tell her that her running-around mother was unavailable on February 13th.

It took weeks of gathering my courage before I sat Jackie down. "Honey," I said, "You know how people ask me to speak a long time ahead?" "Yes, ma'am," she replied. "Well, I've been asked to go to Miami to lead a prayer retreat. They asked me over a year ago. And, it's for February 13th through the 15th. I'm so sorry, but it can't be cancelled now. You do understand, don't you, honey?" I asked.

"Yes, Mama, I do understand," Jackie said. "Of course, it is the most important day in my life . . ." I felt like a worm.

A week or so later, Jennifer came dashing into the house. "Oh Mama," she said, "the Valentine Banquet is going to be wonderful this year!"

Jennifer had just come into her own. Having a beautiful big sister is very difficult if you're spindly-legged and have a nose practically rotting off from sunburn from living in the community swimming pool. But she had begun to blossom. She had wowed us all, including the judges, at the Miss Merry Christmas Pageant and was crowned Queen. She had been elected cheerleader; she served on the youth council at church. She had also discovered boys and loved them. We were holding the line on dating, much to her dismay.

She had just attended youth council and was describing the plans for the banquet. "Best of all," she said, "Roger Vincent has asked me to go to the banquet! Please, Mama!"

Oh, dear. Roger was one of my weak spots. I adored him, and Jennifer was right. It was time to let her have her first date, but I was not going to be at home!

I was furious with the Lord. "You knew this was a weekend I needed to be at home," I told Him. "How could you mess up like this!" My attitude was terrible. It got much worse. I tried to pray about it. I'd start asking the Lord to forgive me and to give me a sweeter spirit. But I'd end up saying, "Lord, I can't believe you'd let this happen. My girls need me that weekend . ." I'd be off again!

Reading the Bible always strengthens me, especially Psalms, so I'd read. But I'd come across "fire-brand" verses that would set me off: "Lord, why have you turned a deaf ear to me?" "Yeah!" I'd echo David, "Why have you, Lord?"

My mind said, "You want to serve the Lord, but with no sacrifice. You have had it easy. At the first demand, you fold." My heart refused to recognize any of those truths.

I just knew God would stop the Florida meeting. Just as He supplied the ram for Abraham's sacrifice, at the very last minute, He would stop my meeting. I even suggested to Him that He could set Miami afloat in the Caribbean and sweep it down below Cape Horn.

February came and nothing happened, except that my attitude got worse. I cried a lot. Finally, February 13th arrived, cold and drizzly. As I boarded Jehosaphat, our van, the drizzle turned to freezing sleet. "Great!" I muttered. The weather matches my mood." I drove to the airport, fussing every mile.

I bypassed the ticket desk and went straight to boarding. I had a good view of the runways outside the terminal. The sleet continued to pepper down.

Only minutes before the flight was to go, I approached the agent at the desk. "Is the flight going to be very late?" I asked.

"Well, as a matter of fact, the plane is on the ground in Memphis. Mechanical problems. I was preparing to cancel," he informed me.

"Cancel? I have a meeting I must attend!" I didn't even think of this as being my way out!

I do have a flight leaving in one hour with one stop," the agent said. "But it's full."

"Well, you find a place for me," I demanded arrogantly, slamming my ticket on the counter.

What had I become? The Lord had blessed me and instead of growing stronger and sweeter, I had become demanding and ugly. How I must grieve Him! I went to my seat, however, with the same haughty attitude.

The announcement was made that the flight had been cancelled. Many scurried to the counter trying to make new plans. The next flight came in. The passengers boarded. The ticket agent called my name. "Do you have any luggage other than that bag?" he asked, pointing to my carry-on.

"No, this is it," I replied. The summer before I had gone to Glorieta Baptist Conference Center to teach during WMU Week. My luggage had gone to beautiful Hawaii for six glorious days in the sun. I'd learned to carry my luggage.

"You may board," he said. "There's only one seat left, the window seat on the front row."

You might expect that I boarded the plane thanking God for a miracle. I didn't deserve the seat. I had been hateful to the agent. I was traveling on a super-saver ticket, and I had the last seat—in first class! Instead, the higher the plane rose in the sky, the better I thought the Lord could hear me. So I sat there in the spacious front seat and went over the whole sorry mess again, blaming God for everything.

All at once, I *felt* the Lord lower the boom. All right, it could have been an air pocket, but the Lord did it. Enough! He allowed me to see the situation through His eyes.

If I had gone to Samford with Jackie I would have driven her wild. I would have peeped in the little glass at the top of the door; I would have looked through key holes. Everytime she went to a different room, I would have been at her heels saying, "How did you do?" The only thing I could do for my little girl was pray that she would do her very best. And God was sending me to a prayer retreat. I would be surrounded by several hundred prayer warriors to pray with me for Jackie.

On Saturday night when I called, I asked, "How did you do?" Jackie said, "Oh, Mama. I did better than I ever have in my life! I was to play only a couple of measures of the Mozart, but they didn't stop me and I played it all the way to the end."

"I had no problems with the sight-reading and the theory was a cinch! They said I'd be hearing from them, that I had one of those scholarships! I don't understand what happened . . ."

"Oh, I do, Jackie," I interrupted, "all of us prayed for you."

Then the Lord turned my eyes toward Jennifer. It was time for Jennifer to have her first date. What better place to have it than at our church Valentine Banquet. She'd be surrounded by people who loved her, who had helped us raise her. Her own daddy would be helping with the serving. Jackie would be there to be sure that she didn't paint herself up like Jezebel. I had ironed her long formal gown four times before it was just right. She was going with the finest young man in Columbiana.

The main problem, I realized, was that I didn't want to miss the fun. But Jen would fill me in for days and days.

I thanked the Lord for our two fine girls, and I cried out of sheer gratitude for God's goodness to us. Then I realized I was not ready for that prayer retreat. I took out my books and started working. I had to get ready, because I realized something else. God knew that it hurt me to be away from my family at a time like this. He would bring much good from this weekend. I knew that something wonderful was going to happen!

When we stopped in Orlando, only one person got off—the person sitting next to me. I barely noticed his departure, since I was so busy. Do you know who got on that plane and sat next to me all the way to Miami? Burt Reynolds!

I have always said, "You can't outgive God!"

God, I know that you think
This child will never learn.
I'm sorry it takes me so long.
I struggle on my own,
I do in my strength,
No help is needed from you.

God, I know you grow weary
This child will never learn.
I'm sorry my spirit is weak.
I truly want to love you
With all of my heart,
But selfish and willful am I.

God, your patience must be gone
This child will never learn.
I thrash and kick just like Paul.
But when the light dawns
I fall at Your feet
And somehow You use me again.

I don't deserve You,
I never will.
But freely you give
and give
and give.

*The vote was 12 to 0 to go to New Mexico. Even I
had voted to go to New Mexico, and I knew better!*

And the Walls Came Tumbling Down

"You have been assigned to the Indian Pueblo in Taos, New Mexico," read our Acteens Activators assignment letter. I refused to believe it. I called Esther Burroughs at the Home Mission Board. Part of her job was to assign Acteens Activators teams.

"I was very specific," I explained to Esther, "about our assignment. This will be our first Acteens Activators trip. We don't have any money. We could never get to New Mexico. I asked to go to the World's Fair in Knoxville, Tennessee."

"I know you did, Barbara, but somebody has to go to Taos. They haven't had a Bible school in years. The home missionaries, Bennie and Edna Romero, are so discouraged. Please pray about it," Esther pled.

Reluctantly, I agreed to pray. Reluctant characterized my feelings about Acteens Activators. Acteens Activators was a new program dreamed up by the National Acteens Consultant, Beverly Sutton. I knew Beverly, she was a good friend. I also knew she has a wild, creative mind. I liked SMAY (Summer Missions Activities for Youth). We had gone SMAY, which was coed, to Chicago, to Kansas City, to migrant camp.

Acteens Activators was different. A church, association, or state team applied to their state WMU. If approved, the application went to the national WMU office. If approved, it was sent to the Home Mission Board for assignment. A minimum of 50 hours of training was required.

I had been persuaded to send in our application by Ann Brack, the Alabama Acteens consultant. Alabama had never had an Acteens Activators team. In 1982, Alabama sent out two teams; our church team from Columbiana, and an associational team from Etowah. We applied to go to Knoxville, Tennessee, to the World's Fair. I had been assured that we would be assigned to the place we chose.

Then came the bombshell letter. Taos! We didn't have the money to go that far, but I already knew about God's provisions. Another problem made Taos the most unlikely place for us.

When on staff at Glorieta Baptist Conference Center the summer after college, I worked with a Pueblo Indian girl, Louisa, who had also been on the staff. She was from Santa Clara Pueblo and life on that peaceful, slow-moving Pueblo was distinctly different from noisy, busy Glorieta. Louisa had three roommates in crowded Yucca Hall. God spared her from having me as a roommate, but I was just down the hall, and I determined in my heart that Louisa and I would be friends.

She just wanted to be left alone. I denied her that privilege. I'd stick my head in the door and ask her to go to Santa Fe or to play softball or to hike. She'd put her head under the covers and try to ignore me. Sometimes I'd even crawl up on the top bunk with her, even put my arm around her.After about two weeks, Louisa ran away. It was nearly 100 miles through terrible terrain to Santa Clara, and she walked every step.

"It was so noisy at Glorieta," she explained. "People were everywhere. One girl even climbed up on my bunk."

I repented of my sins, and asked the Lord to give me a chance to see Louisa and ask her forgiveness. The summer was nearly over when a bus-load of Alabamians came for Sunday School Week. They asked if any of the Alabama staffers would like to go with them to the Indian Pueblos. "Me!" I caroled. The Lord had made a way!

When we arrived at Santa Clara Pueblo, I anxiously searched for Louisa. No sign. I had rehearsed what I would say, very softly and calmly: "Louisa, I didn't mean to worry you. I just wanted to be friends." With one eye toward the adobe buildings, I admired the beautiful black pottery distinctive of Santa Clara. It was very expensive. I put down the $40 ashtray I was examining. Then I saw Louisa! Forgetting all my rehearsals, I screamed her name. She ran, disappearing into one of the buildings. I could have kicked myself! Instead, I pled with the Lord for one more chance

At the end of the summer my parents came to drive me home. I took them to Santa Fe to see the beautiful, historic city. We went to the Plaza where the Indians bring their wares to sell. I tried to persuade my daddy to buy a piece of Santa Clara pottery. "I almost had a friend from Santa Clara," I told him. When he saw the prices, he decided I didn't need a piece of the pottery. We left the Plaza and were walking toward the car when someone caught my arm. It was Louisa! Before I could speak, she pushed a package into my arms and fled.

Inside the package was an exquisite black pottery bowl. My breath caught, and then my heart. I knew Louisa had forgiven me. She wanted to be my friend.

That day in Santa Fe, I promised the Lord I wouldn't mess up His Indian work, and now the Home Mission Board was trying to send us to the only Pueblo more conservative than Santa Clara. It was not until we went to Taos, however, that I discovered that Louisa is Edna Romero's cousin, raised in the same home. Edna's mother, Rose Naranjo, famous Santa Clara potter, had made the bowl I've treasured all these years.

When the Acteens met the following week, I shared Esther's assignment with them. I had guessed their response. They had been excited about going to the World's Fair.

"We can't go," stated Jennifer, "we don't have enough money." (This kid is amazingly like her mother!) "How far is Mexico, anyway?" asked Mandy. "*New* Mexico," I replied. "Let's vote by secret ballot," demanded Donnalee. "We do want to go where God wants us to go," reminded Patty.

We prayed and voted by secret ballot. The vote was 12 to 0 to go to New Mexico. Even I had voted to go to New Mexico, and I knew better!

That first Acteens Activators trip tested us in many ways, but the joy far outweighed the trials. We drove over 800 miles the first day to Oklahoma City. God had an angel, Dorothy Loper, waiting for us. She fed us and bedded us down and got us on our way the next day. She did this all three years we went to Taos. Greater love hath no Acteens leader. When we reached Glorieta, Ginny Hendricks took us in. God is so good.

We reached Taos the third day. Taos Pueblo is virtually unchanged from 700 years ago. There are now doors and windows on the first two floors, but the two massive five-story adobe apartment buildings still house the same families. They can never be sold. Electricity and running water are forbidden. The water supply is a clear, sparkling stream that flows through the Pueblo. Towering over the Pueblo and the town of Taos is the mountain, surely one of the most beautiful in the world. And surrounding the Pueblo is a massive wall, to keep us out, and the Indians in.

The missionary family met us at the little Baptist Mission which was outside the Pueblo. They became our family. Bennie

Romero is full-blooded Taos Indian. His mother lives inside the Pueblo. Edna Romero is originally from Santa Clara Pueblo. They met when Edna's father came to pastor the Indian mission at Taos. The Indian mission became our home for the week. We pitched our sleeping bags between the pews and the wall on the left side of the sanctuary. The concrete was hard and cold, but contrary to my expectations, the Indians were warm and loving. They poured into the little mission. The walls could not hold them. Five years earlier at their last Bible school, they enrolled 10. We had 62 the first day! God opened the doors because so many were praying for us. No one knew that better than I.

The last day was filled with excitement. All of the children joined us to travel up Taos Mountain, forbidden to outsiders, to a beautiful canyon. We had a cookout, played games, and told stories. Jennifer etched her name in Taos lore when 17-day-old Juniper choked on her bottle and stopped breathing. Juniper's mother began wailing; Jennifer raced to her and saw the infant's little blue face. She immediately began mouth-to-mouth resuscitation. Precious seconds later, Juniper started breathing.

That night the people poured in for the program. Our hearts were thrilled as the children sang and recited. The children hugged us and cried and invited us to come back.

We did go back the next summer. All of us knew our work had just begun. Jennifer Joiner, Donnalee Davis, Donna McDaniel, and I returned along with first-timers Stuart Calvert, Pam Burquez, and Tracy Lowe.

Even though the governor of Taos (all the Pueblos have their own independent governments) would not excuse the children from summer school to go to Bible school, even though he would not give teacher Edna Romero time off, Bible school flourished. We went home, however, without seeing a single decision made. Again the children begged us to come back; again the Acteens promised they would, but I said no.

The summer of 1984 was NAC—the National Acteens Convention. Columbiana Acteens had gone to every NAC: to Glorieta, to Memphis, and to Kansas City. I was determined they would go to the fourth NAC in Fort Worth. I had to go. I had written the material: the Bible studies, the Star Kingdoms, the opening theme interpretations for each session. I was leading one of the Star Kingdoms and Jennifer had been asked to do the theme interpretations. No matter how hard I pleaded, the Acteens were unmovable. They wanted to go back to Taos and to NAC as well! Finally, we decided to go to Taos and come back to NAC. We did not have the money to do that, but we asked God to provide one more time. He did. For the third year, Margaret Stinson Lyon, my guardian angel, matched our church's contribution. Thank God for Margaret.

Six Acteens Activators returned to Taos. Missy Vick was the only newcomer. We needed all the advantages we could get, however. Before we reached Little Rock, problems began. The van died. Ray Hogue, the manager of Family Time Rentals in Forrest City, Arkansas, pulled over and hopped out of his truck. As he came toward us, I noted his long hair and beard, his shirt unbuttoned to his waist, his sandals. Mandy Vick said, "It's Jesus!" And believe me, Ray did save us! Five hours later, we were on our way, but without air-conditioning. The rest of the trip we called the van the Sputtering Warrior, Sput for short. We reached Oklahoma City at two o'clock in the morning. Dorothy Loper was waiting for us, as usual.

Finally, in Taos, the mission family welcomed us back as old friends. They serenaded us in Kiowa as well as their native Tiwa. Each member came forward and hugged and kissed us. They are such precious people!

We had our best Bible schools. Nearly 70 came every day. The children learned all the salvation passages and listened eagerly as we explained them. On the final day 16 people made professions of faith! The walls had come tumbling down! We rejoiced at what God had done.

At the end of the Bible school program, Bennie Romero preached a fine sermon. In his closing he paid tribute to the Alabama Acteens by saying, "These Alabama Acteens walk to the same drum beat as we do."

As we left Taos the next day, we knew that we would not be back. God had performed miracles to let us come three years. He had allowed us to see part of the harvest. All of us knew that Taos would forever be part of our heart.

We joined our junior high Acteens in Fort Worth. They had traveled with leader Glenn Milstead and Jackie Joiner Vansant driving. It was Jackie's third NAC. She had been invited as a former Acteens National Advisory Panelist.

Jennifer did a fantastic job with the theme interpretations. And we all marveled at the nearly 15,000 Acteens from all 50 states, plus Canada, Panama, and Puerto Rico. We soared together. What joy to soar to Taos Mountain and to the stars! And to see walls come tumbling down in both places.

The mountain holds the peoples' hearts,
Its spirits rule their lives.
The snow topped peak in summer hot,
Beckons them to forests deep.

The mountain holds the peoples' hearts,
It's sacred ground to them.
Its deep green canyons with sparkling steams,
Pulls them to this beautiful glades.

The mountains hold the Acteens' hearts,
Its people are what we love.
Mountains and walls can shut people out,
But love scales the loftiest heights.

And the walls came tumbling down!
Hallelujah!

"I'm going to Puerto Rico and the Dominican Republic," I informed the travel agent. She was not impressed. "How nice," she yawned.

Spanish Visas and Military Escorts

The pilot burst out of the cockpit. He dashed to the door of the plane and swung it open. Ground crew pushed the staircase into place and 12 splendid soldiers marched to the stairs, 6 on either side. The pilot came to my front-row seat, took my arm, and led me to the door. He made a sweeping motion with his right arm indicating I should descend. I walked down the stairs. As I reached the ground, all 12 soldiers snapped to attention and saluted. I felt their gesture called for something on my part, so I gave a queenly nod.

How had I fallen into this diverse temptation? It began with a phone call on a lovely spring day in 1980. The voice on the other end of the line asked, "Barbara, what are you doing the last two weeks of March next year?"

"To whom am I speaking?" I inquired.

"Jean Richardson," she answered. "I am WMU director for Puerto Rico. We are planning to have a women's retreat next March and we'd like for you to be our speaker."

Puerto Rico! Frantically, I tried to remember its exact location in the Caribbean. This must be a prank call. Puerto Rico could do much better than Barbara Joiner!

"Jean," I cagily replied, "where are you calling from?"

"San Juan," she answered.

"That's in Puerto Rico!" I replied.

"I know. Can you come here to Puerto Rico?"

I grabbed the calendar. "I can if you're sure you want me."

"We do. You'll be hearing from me about everything, the arrangements, all of it," she said, laughing.

I could not believe it! I called Homer immediately. "Homer,

I've been invited to Puerto Rico to speak at a women's retreat! Can you believe it?"

"No," he calmly replied. "Are you sure? Why don't you wait until you get a letter before you get too excited. And don't tell anybody until you're sure."

I hung up, called my ten closest friends and said, "I'm going to Puerto Rico, I think!"

Sure enough, a letter came with the official invitation. Jean instructed me to buy my airplane ticket to San Juan and to let her know the cost. Before I had time to call for reservations, however, I received a call via Halo Network.

Halo Network is the special name given to missionary transmissions by two-way radio. The missionary contacts a person with shortwave equipment, and that person patches in a phone call. It works just like a CB radio. Pat and Sue McFadden, Southern Baptist missionaries in the Dominican Republic, had such a two-way station setup. They radioed someone in Birmingham who patched in a telephone call to me.

Sue McFadden said, "Barbara, we heard you are coming to Puerto Rico next March."

"I really think I am, Sue," I said.

"Puerto Rico is right next door to us in the Dominican Republic. Can you come over for a few days, maybe speak at a couple of things?" she asked.

"Oh, I'd love that, Sue," I said.

"Work it out and let us know dates and times. You would fly into Santa Domingo and we'd meet your flight," she added.

Puerto Rico *and* the Dominican Republic! My cup was running all over the place! I called a travel agent. I had never used a travel agent, but I had never gone to Puerto Rico and the Dominican Republic. I didn't want to do anything dumb.

"I'm going to Puerto Rico and the Dominican Republic," I informed the travel agent. She was not impressed. "How nice," she yawned.

Finally, we worked out flights. "Now what do I need to go to these places, what kinds of papers and shots and such?" I asked.

"My dear," the travel agent replied, "you are not going to darkest Africa. Puerto Rico may someday be our 51st state and the Dominican Republic is right next door."

"But we send foreign missionaries to the Dominican Republic," I argued. "Are you sure I don't need a visa?"

"I am a specialist in travel," she pointed out. I believed her.

A few weeks before my departure, another Halo network call came. This time Pat McFadden talked to Homer. When I got home that night Homer told me about the call. "It was hard to hear Pat," he said. "His voice would drift in and out. But here's what I think he said. Sue has broken her mix master. Can you bring her a new one? And she's out of peanut butter and cocoa."

"I know this sounds crazy," Homer continued, "but he said something about putting the beaters in your shoes."

"It does sound crazy," I agreed.

Pat had said that Sue's mix-master was broken. "Go to K-Mart and get a small hand mixer. In order to get it into the country, put a little jar of peanut butter or a small can of cocoa on top. Wrap up the mixer, put the beaters in a pair of shoes. Maybe they will ignore the mixer and take the peanut butter or cocoa," Pat further instructed.

Not knowing the real situation, I got a big mixer. Homer works for an institutional grocery supply company. He brought home a gallon of peanut butter and a three-pound can of cocoa. I also bought some surprises for Easter baskets for Michael and Amy McFadden and a few other trinkets. I ended up with a suitcase of clothes and a suitcase full of stuff for Sue.

The departure day finally came. I left home before the sun rose but by 3:00 P.M. I was on the ground in beautiful San Juan, Puerto Rico. Jim and Pat Wright, Southern Baptist missionaries to Puerto Rico, met my plane. They and their two sons took me to dinner. Afterward, they delivered me to a plush hotel with tropical flowers blooming in the lobby. My room had a gorgeous view of the white beaches and the breath-taking Caribbean.

The next morning, It was time to go to the interior to the conference center. The ride was fascinating. Orchids were hanging from tree branches, other exotic blossoms everywhere, colorful birds, verdant forests, cascading waterfalls: Puerto Rico is beautiful beyond words.

The conference center, actually a two-story house, had just been purchased. This was its first meeting, and what a meeting it was! Both Spanish-speakers and English-speakers attended. Rosa Martinez was the invited Spanish-speaker. I was the English. When I spoke to the whole group, Rosa translated. We were also roommates.

She said to me, "What is in that suitcase?" pointing to the one filled with Sue's stuff.

"Oh, that's some things I'm taking to my friend, Sue McFadden, in the Dominican Republic. I'm going there after this meeting is finished," I explained.

"Barbara, you can't carry things into the Dominican Republic. They will think you're bringing in merchandise to sell on the black market. What do you have in there?" she asked.

When I told her, she said, "You cannot take those things in. You will be in big trouble! Believe me, I know."

Just because she had traveled extensively in the Caribbean, and had once lived in Cuba, Rosa thought she knew everything!

The meeting came to an end. It had been a wonderful, responsive gathering; we hated to leave. Jean Richardson escorted Rosa and me back to the beautiful hotel. After dinner, we returned to our room, exhausted from the meeting and the traveling. Once more, however, Rosa tried to persuade me to send my contraband bag back home. When I refused to do so, she said, "Let me see your passport. At least I can check it to be sure all is in order."

"Passport?" I don't need a passport. I asked the travel agent; I even argued with her about it," I said.

"Of course you need a passport, for goodness sake!" Rosa exclaimed. "Oh, dear, you are in bad trouble!"

"Rosa, surely there must be some mistake. A passport is not required for the Dominican Republic," I pointed out.

She went to the phone and called the associate to the area director for the Caribbean who lived in San Juan. I was informed by Dr. Graves that I did indeed need a passport.

"Is there anything that can be done at this late date?" I implored.

"When were you to go to the Dominican Republic?" he asked.

"Early Monday morning," I replied.

"If the government offices were open we might try for an emergency visa. I doubt if they'd consider yours an emergency. However, even if you had a late flight Monday, all offices are closed for a religious holiday," he explained.

"Any other way out?" I inquired.

"If a lawyer could be found, and there is no Baptist lawyer that we know of on the island, he might be able to draw up a sworn statement that might be accepted," he said.

"How much?" I asked.

"Maybe $100 or so, during office hours. Barbara, it's hopeless. I'm sorry, but my advice is for you to change your reservations and go on home," he said.

Oh, no! I was sunk! I could have choked that smug, know-it-all travel agent! I turned to Rosa, "You were right, friend. I can't go to the Dominican Republic."

"Can't go?" Rosa's dark eyes flashed. "Aren't you the woman who wrote in *The Dynamic Woman* about God opening doors?"

"Well, yes," I mumbled.

"Aren't you the woman who wrote the Week of Prayer for Home Missions programs entitled "Go Forward!" she added.

"I . . . am," I admitted.

"Then go forward," she cried. "All things are possible! You can do it!"

"Right!" I responded. I picked up the list of numbers I had in case of an emergency. Beatrice Duffer who worked at the seminary was first on the list. I'd try her. I dialed and she answered.

"Beatrice, please tell me you know a Baptist lawyer," I pled.

"Barbara, we've prayed for a Baptist lawyer, but we don't have one yet. What have you done?" she asked anxiously.

"Nothing, except I don't have a passport to go to the Dominican Republic," I moaned.

"Wait a minute," she replied. "Someone is moving in upstairs and they have a lot of books. Hold on." In a few minutes she was back. "Barbara, you're not going to believe this, but the man is a lawyer, a Baptist lawyer! I gave him your number. Hang up, he'll be calling any minute!"

And he did, but he spoke no English! Rosa had gone to sleep. All of my hissing did not wake her up. I said everything I knew to say to the lawyer. I spelled my name. I gave him my address. I told him when I was born. I told him I was going to the Dominican Republic to speak, but I had no papers. "Can you make papers?" I asked slowly. "*Sí*," he replied. "How much?" I asked. "Fifteen dollar?" he inquired. "I can do that!" I exulted.

He gave me an address in San Juan and said, "Three o'clock Sunday." "I can do that." I said again.

I hung up the phone with much hope in my heart and much trepidation. I had done all I knew to do, I went to sleep.

The next morning Rosa left for the US with great concern. Ben and Carole Smith came to pick me up to go to church and spend the day with them. Ben had grown up in Columbiana and I love him dearly. He was working in Puerto Rico. They are a fine young couple with three adorable children. God is so good to His children; the Smiths were just what I needed that day. We went to Calvary Baptist Church then home for a delicious lunch and a good time of fellowship.

I explained what had been happening. Ben said, "Barbara, that lawyer will not show, and no lawyer has ever done anything for $15!" But he agreed to find the street corner specified. We arrived shortly before three o'clock. Shortly after three o'clock, a young man hurried to the corner.

"*Senora* Barbara Joiner?" he asked.

"Yes, I mean, *sí*," I stammered.

He pulled out an impressive looking legal document. He pointed to a place for me to sign. I realized then that the paper was completely in Spanish! The only thing I recognized was "Yo, Barbara Joiner." I signed and he signed. I gave him $15 and he kissed me on both cheeks.

The next morning I went to the airport very early. At the counter marked "Passports," I handed my document to the man on the other side. He read and I prayed. When he finished, he placed the document on the counter, clicked his heels together, and saluted! I was completely baffled, but it seemed that the document was acceptable. The ticket agent came around the counter, tagged both my suitcases, picked them up, and indicated that I was to follow him. He took me down the corridor, outside the building, and right up the steps into a plane. "Oh, Lord, I hope this is the plane to Santa Domingo," I prayed.

The agent buckled me into the seat on the front row, placed my luggage in a compartment, gave me a soda, saluted, and left. I sensed for the first time how Abraham must have felt going out he knew not where.

Thirty minutes later the rest of the passengers boarded. The pilot came by to see if I needed anything. We took off for the brief flight to the Dominican Republic. Thank goodness!

After I deplaned with much pomp and circumstance, the pilot guided me, with my luggage in his hands, to the terminal. For the first time I observed baggage search and removal, but the pilot took me past all that turmoil to a reception room. I sat there after he left; my heart was beating wildly.

Suddenly Pat and Sue McFadden burst into the room. "Why are you here?" they demanded.

"I have no idea. Let's just leave. I'll explain everything when we get to your home," I said.

When we reached their home, I explained all I knew. Pat read my document and began to laugh.

"Barbara, what a document!" Pat said. "You got the royal treatment because this paper says you are here at the express invitation of El Presidente!"

And that, my friends, is why there is still plenty of peanut butter and cocoa in the Dominican Republic!

Sometimes I forget that you rule the Heavens,
That every flight is in your mighty hands.
If you count every sparrow that falls on earth,
You'll surely take care of me.

Sometimes I forget that the oceans and seas are
yours,
You can calm the turbulent storm.
If you count every sparrow that falls on earth,
You'll surely take care of me.

Sometimes I forget you're always here with me,
I'm never alone wherever I go.
If you count every sparrow that falls on earth,
You'll surely take care of me.

Sometimes I forget that you speak Spanish, Lord,
You put the very words in that lawyer's mouth.
If you count every sparrow that falls on earth,
You'll surely take care of me.

The night before we left for Jamaica we discovered that we couldn't carry our 100 boxes of matches unless they were already struck and partially burned.

No Problem in Jamaica

By 1986 we had fielded four Acteens Activators teams, three trips to Taos, New Mexico, and one to Shrewsbury, Massachusetts. A new program was begun that year, Acteens Activators Abroad. Five teams from all over the Southern Baptist Convention were chosen: Phoenix, Arizona; Milton, Florida; Hendersonville, Tennessee; Macon, Georgia; and Columbiana, Alabama, were selected to inaugurate the new program. Four of the teams were assigned to Jamaica, including us.

Jamaica! Discovered by Columbus in 1494, the third largest of the Caribbean Islands, it is considered by many to be the most beautiful of them all.

Jamaica! The island of No Problem. Easy going people populate the isle. Jamaica's first people were Indians. However, most of them perished years ago due to the cruel Spanish taskmasters. African slaves were brought over in the 1600s. The English gained control of Jamaica in the 1800s and they made it a crown colony in 1866. English influence is still predominant. English is the national language. The people are a blend of many races and they are beautiful, warm, and gracious.

The Caribbean Publishing House sent us materials to prepare. The incredible team worked as hard as any Acteens Activators team ever: Shelley Davis, Janet Pate, Melissa Vick, Amanda Vincent, Rebecca Vincent, Stuart Calvert, and me.

I made sure that I knew what papers we needed. Stuart and I needed Passports. The Acteens needed certified birth certificates.

We arrived in Montego Bay, Jamaica, on July 11. We were hustled to a waiting bus going to Ocho Rios. For 3½ hours we rode along the coastal highway. We passed mansions, plantations, millionaires' hide-a-ways, and shanties. The Caribbean with its many hues of blue and green captivated us. At the luxurious Hotel Americana in the beautiful tourist resort of Ocho Rios, we were treated to a fantastic buffet under the stars on the terrace dining room.

The next morning we attended orientation led by the Foreign Mission Board. There were 262 volunteers from all over the United States. Twenty-seven were Acteens Activators and their leaders. We were assigned to work in 84 churches in Vacation Bible Schools and evangelistic services.

At the end of orientation, the Columbiana team loaded into a diesel van which had to be driven on the wrong side of the road, British style! I drove to Passley College in Port Antonio which was home for all of us working in Northeast Jamaica. I retired when we reached Port Antonio and Stuart drove the rest of the week. She loved it (I suspect she drives on the wrong side of the road in the United States!).

At Passley College we shared the third floor with the Tennessee Acteens Activators and the California Baptist College "New Americans," a wonderfully talented singing group.

We ate in the college cafeteria which had, naturally, Jamaican cooks. The taste sensations were anything but natural. We were served two meals a day. Every night the entree was goat. By midnight we had settled into our screenless rooms and sunk into our 1/2-inch mattresses along with assorted moths and other flying creatures. We had the loveliest view of the Caribbean from every window.

On Sunday morning we were off to our first assignment. Bible schools did not begin until Monday, but we went to visit the church where our morning Bible school would be. We drove along the northern coast 1 1/2 hours to the very tip of Jamaica to Belle Castle.

Back at Passley College, Bob Bishop, from Chiefland, Florida, our area coordinator, asked us if we would be willing to do a second Bible school in the afternoon. We accepted readily, and we got busy multiplying our crafts.

Early Monday morning, we returned to Belle Castle. We came to love the sounds of Belle Castle: the pledge to their flag—"We pledge the strength and vigor of our bodies . . ."—and their national anthem—"Jamaica, Jamaica, Jamaica, land I love!"—and the children. We averaged 229 children each day.

We learned about different lunches. On Monday we had green coconut jelly via machete from one of the church members and potent June plum juice from Kathleen Wilson, the pastor's wife. Kathleen accompanied us up a long mountain trail, through tropical rain forest, to our afternoon Bible school at Top Moro. It was their first Bible school ever, and it was the poorest church in Belle Castle Circuit. Twelve poles topped with a rusty patchwork tin roof, scraps of tin along the sides, and three rough, wooden benches made up the tiny church. The village was removed from the world. Perched at the summit of the Blue Mountains, the scenery was spectacular.

The people observed us solemnly for about ten minutes. We knew it was our time of judgement. Then Mrs. Stewart came bustling out with a fiery drink made of roots that made our eyes water. Nobody batted an eye. We all drank and thanked. Each day that week Mrs. Stewart went all over the village rounding up enough ice and glasses for us to have refreshment.

The first day at Top Moro we packed 38 people into the tiny room. By the end of the week we had 88. We never saw where most came from. They looked Indian. It was not until the end of the week, after being accompanied each day by at least one nervous member of Belle Castle, that we were told that Top Moro *was* Indian, one of the remnants of the early island Indians who had turned cannibalistic. We saw no evidence of that while we were there. Later, Homer remarked that they missed the meal of a lifetime when they failed to get me in their cooking pot.

The week flew by. On Wednesday, my group, all 85 of them that day, made sheep. That meant 85 of everything except 170 eyeballs, 170 pupils, 170 ears, and 340 legs. We had glue on every single piece. I vowed never to do any kind of animal for crafts ever again. Stuart and Melissa never want to see a burned match again after making matchstick crosses. Stuart doesn't know the half of it. The night before we left for Jamaica we discovered that we couldn't carry our 100 boxes of matches unless they were already struck and partially burned. We had a lighting party that night when we had a million *important* things to do.

When Friday came, we went earlier and carried all our supplies. We would leave all extra supplies at Belle Castle and Top Moro. At Top Moro we had our biggest day and the most poignant moment of the entire week. The Indians, who had been silent until Wednesday, taught us a song. "It makes no difference if you're rich or poor, or black or white . . ." We were holding hands, our eyes met across the tiny room and tears fell. Nothing made a difference. These dear secluded people had become our friends.

After a glass of tamarind seed juice that opened our sinuses, we journeyed back to Belle Castle for commencement. They had made the church beautiful with exotic blossoms. All of the crafts for the whole week were displayed, including 85 sheep. We were thrilled by their presentations and the excellent memorization. Then they surprised us with a special song which they had been working on all week. They sang and danced and the tambourines rang! It was wonderful. This was followed by the children presenting each of us with gifts. They did so with elaborate speeches of thanks which charmed us and touched us deeply.

We went back to Passley College for late supper. We could not eat the curried goat or the cold breadfruit, but we really dug into the bowl of gelatin. Somehow we made it. Our devotional times each night strengthened us spiritually and helped us survive physically, too.

On Saturday, our only free day, we had big plans. We traveled to Port Antonio to the Hotel DeMontevin where the late Errol Flynn's former cook is now chef. We had a five-course meal including the world's best lobster. It made up for all the goat we had tried to eat!

Then we made our first foray to the straw market. Money changed hands very rapidly as souvenirs and presents were purchased. We all loved bargaining. "Too much," we'd say. "No problem," they'd reply.

None of us could put into words what the week had meant to us. I know I counted it all joy. Well, maybe not the curried goat, but that was just a gnat on an otherwise perfect experience. We loved Jamaica and longed to return.

Guess what eight of my senior high Acteens got for Christmas this year. Jamaica! Their parents gave them Jamaica! We are going back this summer, and I cannot wait for this group to taste curried goat!

Beauty beyond measure—
Azure waters lap the shores,
Blossoms perfume the air,
Blue sky meets blue sea,
White sand glistens 'neath the sun.
JAMAICA!

Luxury beyond imagination—
Sprawling plantations stately,
Mansions of every hue,
Hotels boast tropical gardens,
Sail boats skimming the bays,
JAMAICA!

People beyond compare—
Lilting voices singing,
Rhythm sets bodies swaying,
Smiles to set hearts fast beating,
Precious children hugging, loving,
JAMAICA!

Lord,
Thank you for letting us share
With two little corners of
JAMAICA!

*I was going to steamy, sultry Nigeria during the
hottest part of their year, to Communist Ethiopia,
and to primitive Yemen—my three favorite tourist
spots on earth!*

African Safari and Yemen, Too

In 1982, Alabama Baptists entered into partnership with the
West African nation of Nigeria. Nigeria is by far the most popu-
lous nation in Africa. One out of every four sub-Sahara Africans
live in Nigeria which has a population of over 113 million.

Nigeria is the oldest missions field with continuous service for
Southern Baptists. Work began there in 1850, the third country
Southern Baptists entered. The Nigerian Baptist Convention was
organized in 1914. The Nigerian Baptist Convention, the
Nigerians themselves, formulated the plans for the Nigeria-
Alabama partnership. They asked us to send our finest preachers
and musicians to lead in simultaneous revival services all over
the country. Many teams responded during 1983.

In the spring a request came from the Southern Baptist
Mission of Nigeria, the missionaries. They asked me to lead
prayer retreats for them. When Dr. Harrell Cushing, president of
the Alabama Baptist Convention, relayed this message to me, I
responded with my typical vibrant faith.

"Well, I can't go."

"Why not?" asked Dr. Cushing.

"For two reasons," I answered. "In the first place, I'm not spiritually adequate to lead missionaries in prayer retreats."

"We know that," quipped Dr. Cushing.

I continued, "And I know how this partnership works. You
pay your own way. Our oldest daughter, Jackie, is in school at a
Baptist college, Samford University. You don't take any trips with
a child in a Baptist college. Not only that, but she's in their
famed A Cappella Choir, and they're going to Europe on concert
this summer. We are going to have the privilege of paying for

that trip. Not only that, but Jackie has a diamond on her left hand. The wedding is scheduled for next Christmas. She is planning a small wedding with 12 bridesmaids. We'll probably have to sell the homestead to pay for that wedding! Then Jennifer is entering Auburn University the next fall."

"Stop!" Dr. Cushing said. "Just pray about it, Barbara. God has a way of working things out."

My position has always been don't pray unless you're ready to do it God's way! So I procrastinated. I tried to pretend that God knew nothing about the invitation. That sort of subterfuge destroys your prayer life. Finally, one step from telling God, I told Homer. He said, "If God wants you to go, He'll provide the way." He was right, of course.

Then a letter came from Nigeria, from one of my all-time missionary heroines, Anita Roper. She told me to get myself to Nigeria. Her clincher was: "We've forgotten how to laugh. Come help us laugh again."

"I can do that! OK, I'm ready if you are, Lord!" I said to myself.

The Lord was ready. He made the way and I was overwhelmed. I keep forgetting that His resources are inexhaustible!

Three days after I knew I was going to Nigeria, the phone rang. It was Jerry Bedsole in Ethiopia. "Barbara, we've just learned that you are coming to Nigeria in February. The Mission here in Ethiopia would like for you to come from Nigeria over here to speak at our Mission meeting. We'll pay the difference in airfare." Now how did they know I was going to Nigeria? I'd only known three days! And sure, fly on over. It was like flying from Los Angeles to New York City!

I wanted to see Rosie and Jerry and those Bedsole boys. I wanted to see the country I'd prayed for so long. "Sure!" I said. "I'll write all the details," Jerry responded.

Three days later a phone call came from Yemen. Martha Myers, Southern Baptist missionary doctor said, "Barbara, we've heard that you're coming to Ethiopia in March. Can you come on over to Yemen then? We'll pay the difference in airfare."

Now how did they know I was going to Ethiopia? My joy knew no bounds. I was going to steamy, sultry Nigeria during the hottest part of their year, to Communist Ethiopia, and to primitive Yemen—my three favorite tourist spots on earth!

The first order of business was gathering things to carry to the missionaries. I had helped missionaries pack to go out. I knew they counted every can and bag carefully. All those preachers and ministers of music had probably diminished their supplies greatly. I felt compelled to replenish. But what? How? I called one of the pastors from Birmingham who had gone to Nigeria. "Barbara, don't carry anything in! Didn't you hear about the preachers being arrested in Port Harcourt?"

"Yes," I answered, "but they were carrying in those Vienna sausages for their own snacks! If they had been taking them to missionaries, God would have protected them."

The preacher snorted, "Don't do it, Barbara. You'll get into bad trouble."

I called another preacher and got the same advice. Then I remembered that my friend, Maxine Bearden, had gone on one of the teams. "Maxine, I'm going to Nigeria to lead some prayer retreats," I said. "What should I take to the missionaries?"

"Take a canned ham," she responded immediately. "They are so expensive—if you can find one. Take several if you can. Of course, you aren't supposed to take any food in, but wrap it in your clothes. And take a can of shortening so Anita Roper can have fried chicken. Take some mayonnaise and jelly. Jelly is very precious." Maxine is my kind of risk-taking woman!

I started buying immediately. Soon a letter came from Jerry Besdole asking for 50 rolls of film, 100 cassette tapes, and a box of needles to give shots to horses. I added to that list ten pounds of M&Ms for the boys. Some canned bacon and dehydrated strawberries along with some cassette tapes of Christian music were heaped on for Yemen.

Homer looked at the food bank with dismay. "How much can you take?" he asked. I called the travel agent. "One suitcase that weighs no more than 70 pounds," she decreed. "However, you can take a second bag if you're willing to pay the excess baggage fee." "I can do that," I replied.

I packed two huge suitcases so full that three of us sat on the suitcases while Homer closed them. We were sure that each weighed more than 70 pounds. It took the greatest effort for me to lift just one of them. I also had a carry-on that topped 40 pounds, and my purse was a leaden weight.

When February 21, 1984, arrived, my entire family plus a whole gaggle of Acteens escorted me to the airport. Homer and my new son-in-law, Dana Vansant, got those two monster suitcases in the airport. We were making so much noise that the ticket agent was rattled. He loaded my suitcases, both of them on the baggage runway without a question or, praise the Lord, extra charge. I said, "Are those checked all the way through to Lagos, Nigeria?" "Yes, Ma'am," the agent barked, "and you can take your friends and go to the gate." We did.

Before I knew it, we had hugged and kissed and I was on my way to Atlanta. Dear Margaret Burks from Flowery Branch, Georgia, met my plane and escorted me to the International Concourse. She brought an enormous Georgia WMU tote bag full of presents for Anita Roper in Nigeria. It weighed about the same as my carry-on, so I was more-or-less balanced. Soon I boarded my next flight, bound for London.

I had a six-hour layover in London, and I had never been in that fabulous city. I planned to use every minute to see all I could. My husband had said, "Don't wear yourself out in London. Rest. Remember why you're going."

The London weather was dark and stormy. When I asked the airline agent about transportation into the city, he shook his head. "Don't go out into this awful weather. You'll catch your death." He clinched his argument by giving me the key to a room in the adjoining hotel and gave me eight pounds for a meal. I understand that is not common practice. Homer says I attract such kindnesses because I look like I need help!

I went to my free room, had a wonderful hot herbal bath and a five-hour nap. Then I went to the tearoom, had high tea, and boarded my long flight to Lagos, Nigeria. The flight was crowded; there was no sleeping. I thanked the Lord for my wonderful sleep in London for I arrived in Lagos at 6:00 A.M. relatively rested.

I had made the decision to be a gracious traveler. I waited until everyone else had deplaned, then I put on my all-weather coat with its woolly zip-in lining. It had been cold in London and would be in Amsterdam on my way home. I hung my heavy purse around my neck. On top of that went Homer's fine camera. I picked up my two heavy-weight carry-ons and staggered down the aisle. I stepped off the plane a little after 6:00, it was already 126 degrees! I slipped and slid into the airport.

They checked my passport quickly. Up ahead I saw a sight that brought tears to my eyes. Agents were lifting the suitcases and slamming the contents on the counters, looking for contraband. "Oh, no," I said to myself, "they're going to break my jelly!" I immediately started telling the Lord how to handle the situation, "Blind them, Lord!" I suggested.

With a sinking heart I went to the luggage carousel. All around me people were claiming their belongings. Suddenly the carousel ceased to turn, and my bags were not there. I had been told what to do in case my luggage did not come—forget it. You will never see your luggage again in this lifetime. I stood there looking bereft, like I needed help. An Irish woman whose husband was in the oil business in Nigeria came over. "What's wrong, my dear?" she asked. "My luggage did not come," I tearfully related.

She looked over to one side of the building where a splendid young man stood, attired in a fine military uniform arrayed with ribbons and medals. Over his shoulder was slung a highly polished rifle. She motioned to him. Taking my luggage tags from me, she handed them to the young man along with a ten niara note (approximately $13.50). "Go find this luggage," she said to him. Turning to me she said, "I've always wanted to try that!"

Ten minutes later the young man came out, wheeling my two massive suitcases on a trolley. He loaded my carry-on bags and my now soggy coat. He wheeled the whole lot right past the customs' agents with me hot on his heels. I don't know if it was because he was a soldier or security or if you just don't argue with a rifle! He pushed the trolley right out to Anita Roper's car and deposited it all in the "boot" of her automobile.

A month later I returned to the airport in Lagos with a midnight flight to Ethiopia. My luggage was greatly reduced. One big suitcase had been relegated to Anita Roper's storeroom. Both carry-ons had been emptied in Nigeria. I carried Jackie's old yellow suitcase which held that unneeded coat. However, I was also taking in the suitcase of film, cassettes, and long corkscrew needles. Several missionaries in Ethiopia had been detained (that's polite for arrested) for taking in such.

When I boarded the Ethiopian Airline jet, the first face I saw was that of a handsome Ethiopian man, smiling at me from ear-to-ear. I realized it was because I was smiling at him. I love Ethiopians. I claim Sophia Kebede, a former Ethiopian student, as my daughter. Ethiopians are striking people with high foreheads and proud bearing. I had even learned to eat, if not appreciate, their *injera* and *wat*, traditional bread and stew.

My seat was directly behind the Ethiopian gentleman. Gratefully, I saw that no one was seated on my row. Jerry Bedsole had written, "Sleep on the plane. You will arrive at 9:30 in the morning and you will speak for the first time shortly after." I put up the armrests, stretched out with my purse under my head, and closed my eyes.

Tap, tap, tap! It was the Ethiopian gentleman. He was holding a pillow. "This will be much more comfortable," he said in excellent English. I took the pillow, put it on top of my purse, and closed my eyes again.

Tap, tap, tap! Again the Ethiopian gentleman was standing at my row. He was holding a small blanket. He suggested that it would get really cold on the flight. Again I thanked him, thinking I'd never be cold again after a month of Nigerian heat! I stretched the blanket over my legs and closed my eyes. Before I did, I noticed that the woman sitting beside this Ethiopian gentleman had already stretched out with her head in his lap; she was sound asleep. For several delicious hours, I also had a cool nap. Then we landed in the Cameroons and took on one passenger who was assigned to my row. I sat up the rest of the trip.

Hours later we landed in Nairobi, Kenya. The woman with her head in the Ethiopian man's lap sat up and left the plane. I was stunned! I thought she was his wife! He turned and looked at me. My mouth was wide open.

"She was certainly a friendly lady," he observed.

"Friendly, yes; lady, I doubt," I said without thinking. He roared with laughter.

After the flight, now greatly reduced in number, left for Ethiopia, breakfast was served. *Injera* and *wat!* "Would you like this?" I asked my new friend. He had polished his tray already. "Of course," he responded. After finishing my breakfast he asked if I'd like to swap newspapers. I traded my several-days-old paper for his. By the time we reached Addis Ababa, the capital of Ethiopia, we were talking like old friends. We entered the airport together. "Give me your luggage claim and I'll get it while you have your passport checked," he suggested. I had been told not to do that. He handed me his briefcase. "He wouldn't steal my luggage," I said to myself. "I have his briefcase."

I went to passport check. Unlike Lagos, they checked and re-read my tiny passport. Then they went back to page one and re-read as if reading Deuteronomy. I had one eye on the luggage coming in. I saw the Ethiopian gentleman grab my bag. He came toward me. He spoke to the agent in Amharic, the official language of Ethiopia. The agent stamped my passport immediately. Then my friend took my arm and we walked right by the customs' officials who were busy taking whatever they pleased from the suitcases coming through.

We walked out to the waiting area. The Bedsoles, the Groces, and the Waldrons were waiting for me. My new friend looked at my old friends and they recognized each other. The Ethiopian gentleman handed me my suitcase, grabbed his briefcase out of my hands and left. Jerry Bedsole approached me anxiously and asked, "Barbara, what were you doing with that Communist security agent?"

"Communist security agent?" I choked.

"Did you see another Ethiopian on the plane in Western

dress?" Jerry asked. "Or another not loaded down with luggage? He had just his briefcase. Of course, it had his revolvers, his hand grenades, and who-knows-what-else!" I had carried that arsenal all over the airport!

A week later I was back in the airport on my way to Yemen. I had one bag with very little inside. The only contraband was canned bacon, dehydrated strawberries, and Christian music cassettes. I was flying Ethiopian Airline again. It was a small plane. Only three women were on board: the stewardess, an Arab woman whose face was heavily veiled, and me. There were many Arab men in robes. At the last minute, an Ethiopian man in Western-style clothes carrying a briefcase boarded. I knew who he was, but he didn't look in my direction.

After a brief flight across the Red Sea, we landed in Sanaa, Yemen. Once again, I waited for my luggage. As the carrousel began to turn, the waiting passengers started to make gasping sounds. As the bags came toward me I saw that clumps of some gooey substance was deposited on the bags. Finally, my suitcase came into view and I discovered the problem. A goatskin of the famous Yemeni honey had been checked. In the hot cargo bay, it had gotten warm; the bag had spewed out its contents. The entire bag was resting on top of my yellow suitcase. I did not just have clumps of honey; my bag had been baptized! The handle had also come loose. Gingerly, I grabbed the suitcase tilting it away from me. I galloped across the stone floor to a rough wooden table where bags were being examined. As I threw my suitcase on the table, honey gushed toward the agent. "Get that thing out of here," he said. I did.

Sometimes God covers His children like a chicken covers her babies with her wings. Sometimes He covers us with His honey. Whatever it takes to get the job done, He does it.

By this time I understood what had happened. I was going to three of God's most remote outposts to make people laugh. If I had been afraid, I couldn't have done that. Right at the beginning in Nigeria, I saw God at work. He was undeniably there. It would have been inappropriate for me to be afraid. So I walked in faith, in laughter, and in joy!

Glory be to God in the highest!
Thank you for making military men,
All spit and polish—
Rifle at the ready—
That was exactly what I needed!

Glory be to God in the highest
Thank you for the Communist Security Agents,
Helpful and gracious—
Briefcase all loaded—
That was exactly what I needed!

Glory be to God in the highest!
Thank you for making Yemeni honey,
Ooey and gooey—
Spilling from goatskins—
That was exactly what I needed!

Wherever He leads, I'll go.
For He goes before,
He goes alongside,
He goes after to clean up my messes.
Glory be to God in the Highest!

I was so thrilled over my visa, I would have kissed his foot.

On to Yemen

Going to Nigeria, Ethiopia, and Yemen was the miraculous part, but being there was fantastic. I forgot Nigeria's heat even though I discovered why bodies have sweat glands. My eyes were too busy drinking in the sights. Anita Roper, a veteran in Lagos traffic, can join the NASCAR circuit when she retires. As she whizzed through the streets, I saw people everywhere. All seemed to be selling their wares. At every stop, cars were besieged with offers of bananas and pineapples (the best in the world), sandwiches and cakes, television sets and mattresses. You name it, they sell it.

When we reached Yaba, the suburb where Anita lives, GAs were waiting for us. Anita is the Girls' Auxiliary (our Girls in Action) director for Nigeria. They captured my heart as they sang and danced and gave their testimonies.

The next day we were off to the first prayer retreat in Ogbomosho. Traveling up country was a treat; the countryside was beautiful. We rode on modern paved roads through dense jungles and swamps with trees covered with blossoms of every hue. Along the highways people were everywhere, men in long formal robes, women with babies on their backs and loads on their heads. The loads fascinated me. Men carried enormous logs on their heads. Women and children balanced heavy trays filled with vegetables or fruits or any number of things.

We reached Ibadan, the headquarters for the Nigerian Baptist Convention, around noon and lunched in the building. Anita had packed a picnic. She had even arranged a brief audience with Dr. Akande, the head of the Nigerian Convention. He was very gracious.

Then we traveled on to Ogbomosho reaching the beautiful seminary compound by late afternoon. I was welcomed by my hostess at Ogbomosho who is my friend and an Alabama native, Mary Jane Wharton. Mary Jane's duplex was a little bit of America planted in Africa, as is the guest house where we gathered for a Baptist covered-dish supper before beginning the prayer retreat.

The prayer retreat was my reason for being in Ogbomosho, but after the retreat God showed me why I had really come. Missionary Sharron Hawk took me to Kersey's Children's Home. The home was originally begun to care for abandoned children. Today it still cares for such children but also for children who are malnourished. They care for 40 children at a time, accompanied by their mothers or grandmothers and brothers and sisters. They crowd into the tiny assigned cubicle with their own mats, food, and cooking pots.

I saw precious fat children who had been at Kersey's for months and were recovering. I also saw new arrivals with swollen bellies and spindly legs. I saw a little one die in the arms of Ruth Womack as she attempted to feed the babe with an eye dropper. Ruth, now retired as director of Kersey's, is a saint, but she's a tough one for she insists that the mothers attend classes to learn how to feed and care for their babies.

The next day, Mary Jane Wharton and Shirley Gunn took me to Promised Land, the leprosy village. Forty people were already worshiping in the little mud church they had built with their own misshapened hands. They came pouring out of the church to welcome us. Promised Land was Hazel Moon's child; now the lepers call Mary Jane their Mama.

I learned a new meaning to joy; I have never seen such joy. Moses won my heart—no fingers, only one leg, but the most radiant smile. Through an interpreter, he said "When I came to Promised Land, I found that Jesus loves me!"

The singing was accompanied by drums and bells, and the people danced with joy. What matter if they danced on crutches or on hobbled feet!

Promised Land needed a well. I was determined they would have it. Because of people in Alabama and Louisiana and Wisconsin, Promised Land now has that well. Thank you, Lord.

The next prayer retreat was up-country in Zaria.

As we went north we left behind palms, mango, and guava trees. Huge rock mountains dotted the skyline. Fulani tribesmen driving their herds appeared.

At the end of the day we reached Kaduna and the pastors'

school. Fred and Mary Lou Levrets took me to the home of Paul and Faye Burkwall. The Burkwalls, friends already, teach at the school. I helped teach three classes and was asked to speak in chapel twice. Kaduna was one of my favorite places in Nigeria. Fifty tribes were represented, living side-by-side at the school, studying and working together in harmony. They sang in chapel accompanied by jugs, drums, and rattles. The joy was infectious.

Hausa-land is hot. I made a note in the journal I kept that it was 120 degrees at daybreak and so dry I couldn't spit! But the next sentence noted that the frangipani and jacaranda and bougainvillea were breathtaking.

My favorite thing in Kaduna was the church service at the Burkwall's. Eight Fulani young men in the pastors' school came with their newly translated Fulfuldi (the language of the Fulanis) Bibles and a few pages of songs. One student led the service but all shared. The presence of God was evident. From Kaduna we went on to Zaria for the prayer retreat for the area. There was a sweet spirit and we laughed a lot. We also cried as Bert Dyson shared about his and Ruth's leaving their beloved Nigeria to begin work in Sierra Leone.

Jim Johnston showed me his Hausa Printing Headquarters. I wrote in my journal: "If only Jimmy Vick could come help Jim set up the equipment." Jimmy is an outstanding deacon in First Baptist, Columbiana, who teaches printing at our vocational school. That summer our church sent Jimmy to Zaria, Nigeria!

March 3 is my birthday. I awoke *very* homesick. I had decided to tell no one because I didn't want anybody to use their "things" on me. That night I had supper with Don and Ina Frazier. Ina had prepared a feast and we had a wonderful time together. After we finished I thanked her for my birthday dinner. The Kaduna missionaries, not to be outdone, gave me a ten-minute call home. What a perfect birthday gift!

Philip and Sandy Wilson picked me up in Kaduna and we traveled to Jos for the next prayer retreat. I learned to love the Wilsons as we climbed steadily to the plateau town of Jos. Fellow Alabamian, Jane Ellen Gaines, claimed me when we arrived. I felt at home in Jos with another Alabama native, Mike Stonecypher, there as well.

We went to Miango, the Sudan Interior Mission Rest Home, for the prayer retreat. It was cool and rainy. The water could be drunk from the tap. The food was delicious. There were enforced siestas. Best of all, the prayer retreat was fun and funny and uplifting. I was glad to be in that place.

New friend, Lou Ann Nicholson took me to Jos airport to fly

to Lagos on Nigeria Airways. We flew low enough to see the cooking fires in hundreds of villages.

I went to big city churches and bush churches in Nigeria and loved them all. Warmth and welcome as well as exuberant worship characterized the Nigerian church. I felt at home with my brothers and sisters in the Lord.

My biggest disappointment was in not getting to do the prayer retreat in Eku. Their schedule and my flight to Ethiopia were in conflict. With mixed feelings, I left for Ethiopia.

When I arrived in Addis Ababa, Ethiopia, the air was sweet and cool. The high altitude keeps the temperature moderate all year long. Evidences of Communism were everywhere from the huge statue of Lenin to the ever-present hammer and sickle.

Our first task was to try to get a visa from Yemen. The airlines had been most reluctant to route me to Yemen without a visa, and I was told by the Yemini Embassy in Washington, D.C., that the only possibility was to get one in Addis Ababa. Jerry Bedsole and I went to the Legation. "Just be calm, Barbara," he advised. "They will take one look at your honest face and you'll get your visa." Not so. They asked question after question. Things were not going well. Then I said the magic words: "I am a friend of Dr. James M. Young, Jr." One of the officials broke into smiles and explained that Dr. Young had treated his son, and his son was now well and strong. He stamped my passport and I experienced the Yemeni kiss for the first time. He grabbed my hand and kissed it, then stretched his hand to me and I kissed it. We swapped hand kisses three times and ended the ritual by each of us kissing our own hand on the kissing spot. I was so thrilled over my visa, I would have kissed his foot.

My time in Ethiopia was so brief, but we packed it full. I stayed with the Bedsoles but spent time with the Groces; the Waldrons; John Lawrence, the volunteer veterinarian; and Mary Lou Jackson, a journeyman. I'm proud to say that I gave the Lawrence-Jackson romance a good, solid push. They are now Dr. and Mrs. Lawrence and are career missionaries in Ethiopia.

Missionaries were confined to Addis Ababa at that time but I saw Addis. The most joyous experiences were calling on the mother and sisters of my Ethiopian daughter, Sophia Kebede, and Gabre Hiwot, the lawyer who helped Southern Baptists enter Ethiopia. Gabre Hiwot had been jailed for nine years. My Acteens and I had prayed faithfully for his release. It was glorious to see that answer to prayer in the flesh!

Two things I did more than any other. I spoke frequently, even at the international church, and I ate *injera* and *wat!* One day I was served five kinds of the stew. The Bedsole boys sat close to me and ate my portion. I am beholden for life!

To pick one major event in Ethiopia would be difficult. If hard pressed, I'd choose my meeting with Jerry Bedsole and Seleshi. Seleshi, an outstanding young man of faith, shared about the spread of Christianity in Ethiopia. I imagined myself sitting with the Apostle Paul. He had such vision, such courage. He was not afraid of anything—prison or death or dying. It was a profound experience.

After tearful good-byes I flew off to Yemen. Martha Myers and Ethne Stainer met my flight. What a welcome sight to see them waving from the airport roof as I walked off the plane!

I thought I was ready for Yemen, but I was not. The four-hour drive with the steep terraced mountains and deep valleys, villages carved into the sides of the mountains, was spectacular. When I saw our Baptist hospital for the first time, I burst into tears. How long I had prayed for that miraculous hospital!

It was not until four o'clock the next morning when the call to prayer echoed all over Jibla that I knew I was in Yemen for sure and felt the grip of Islam on its people. My resolve to pray for missionaries who work in Muslim countries was intensified.

The missionaries in Yemen are unlike those in other countries. Without contract medical people, the hospital could not function. They are not career or volunteer personnel, they work in Jibla on contract. Ethne Stainer, from Australia, started out as a contract nurse. She is now a Southern Baptist career missionary and one of our best.

The Youngs were home on furlough (my one disappointment) but other fine doctors were holding the fort: Martha Myers, Jean Dickman, and David Young. Some of the most dedicated nurses in the world, some career, some special project, some journeymen, some contract, serve in Yemen. A hospital administrator, Bill Koehn, and a maintenance man, Al Lindholm, keep things operating. These people have to be some of the Lord's finest.

I fell in love with the Yemeni people. Gracious and hospitable, they welcomed me into their homes. Of course, it was because I was with Dr. Martha. They love Martha Myers. Martha is amazing. She eats only if a Yemeni friend or other missionary feeds her. She works at the hospital constantly. The few days I stayed with her I did not see her sleep more than a couple of hours. Her love for the Yemeni people is a tangible thing. If she doesn't work herself to death, she'll someday be the Baptist Mother Teresa.

On Martha's coattails, I climbed to the top of several of those earliest apartment buildings in the world. Up winding stairs, finally emerging into elegant parlors, we would shed our shoes and sit on cushions on lovely Persian rugs. We were served refreshments, bowls of raisins and almonds, brightly wrapped candies, carbonated drinks. On arrival, we were sprayed lavishly with cologne. On leaving, the hand kissing commenced.

We visited the 900-year-old mosque of Queen Arwa guided by one of the Yemeni nurses. We visited the market; we walked down the *wadi*, the dry river bed. We even attended a circumcision party. (It was in honor of, not in witness of, thank goodness!) A feast followed the party and I discovered the delicious seven-layer Yemeni bread called daughter of the pan. I like Yemeni food.

In their homes, the women shed their *sharshiffs* (the two-layer veils). Under the black capes and outer skirts, they wear colorful dresses and a great deal of gold jewelry. Most of the Yemeni people are small and very attractive. The men wear fine, curved daggers called *jambias*. No man would leave home without it.

When it was time to leave for home, the Provosts took my battered bag with zipper now broken, and gave me one of their suitcases. We have swapped back now, and Jackie's old yellow suitcase, has been repaired and has made many more miles.

We were accompanied by missionary Sarah Thomas and my favorite Yemen native, Burud who works in the operating room of the hospital. She decided she was my guardian and helper. Everywhere we went, Burud held my hand. That is the custom in Yemen.

As I boarded my flight to go home, in my heart I continued to hold hands with Burud in Yemen, Seleshi in Ethiopia, Moses in Nigeria, and a whole host of missionaries. God had allowed me to see some of this choice people in their homelands and their chosen lands. I felt anew our kinship as children of the Lord. I had been blessed.

When I returned home, I had a letter from the associate director for the Middle East, Dr. Finlay Graham. He thanked me for encouraging the beleaguered flock in Yemen. He said, "I have heard that you exude the joy of the Lord."

Oh, I hope so, Dr. Graham, I do hope so.

Dear Lord,
Whatever possesses anyone to go to Nigeria,
To suffer the wet and clinging heat,
To wait for malaria, knowing it will come,
To ration every drop of precious boiled
water?
Lord, why do they go?

Dear Lord,
Whatever possesses anyone to go to Ethiopia,
To chance their lives under Communist rule,
To face all the fighting, all of the dying,
To never know what tomorrow might bring?
Lord, why do they go?

Dear Lord,
Whatever possesses anyone to go to Yemen,
To travel to a land hostile to all we believe,
To sever all ties to modern civilization,
To live far beyond all comfort and ease?
Lord, why do they go?

Dear Lord,
Whatever possessed you to go to the cross?
To die for me,
for Nigeria,
for Ethiopia,
for Yemen.
Someone has to tell them,
That's why they go.

Not every situation has been easy or joyful. The sorrow and anxiety have taught me how to pray for miracles. I have learned that lesson well, and I have seen God bring the miracles to pass.

The Main Ingredient Is Joy

Here I am at the last chapter and I have not shared nearly all the joy! I'm looking at notes I've made that are not chapters or even footnotes. They are begging to be told.

I remember when Jackie made her profession of faith in May 1970. Jennifer was in the four-year nursery. Jackie said, "Please let me be the one to tell Jen." After the family was in the car, Jackie said, "Jennifer, today I became a Christian." Jennifer replied, "Oh, my Lord, who am I going to play with now?" Our daughters are our pride and joy, and entertainment!

We love to hear Jackie, a graduate of Samford University with a major in Piano Performance, play. She is pianist at our church and is busy being wife to Dana and mother to five-year-old, Megan, and four-year-old, Dane, the most adorable grandchildren in the world.

Jennifer, our cheerleader from birth, is now busy working as a court reporter for Tyler, Eaton, Morgan, Nichols, and Pritchett in Birmingham. In January 1990, she became Mrs. Terry Lee Ward in the first wedding in our beautiful new sanctuary at First Baptist, Columbiana.

Jennifer cried her heart out the day she started kindergarten. I could not imagine why. She had been excited about going to school. When she controlled her sobs, she explained, "I'll never get enough pickles at kindergarten!" I understood her problem. She went with me when I taught mission studies and she demolished the relish trays at the covered-dish luncheons. When she got home from school that day, I had a jar of gherkin pickles waiting for her after-school snack. She still gets a jar of gherkins and a fresh pineapple in her stocking every Christmas.

Another joyful thing about my life is I have the best, most understanding husband in the world. One Sunday night I overheard Homer and another one of our deacons. The deacon said, "Homer, I know you get tired of Barbara running around all the time!" Wasn't that a lovely way to describe my speaking and teaching! Homer replied, "Well, you know, I feel like Barbara has something to share."

That night at home, I said to him, "Honey, I was in the kitchen tonight, and I heard what you said about my having something to share. I couldn't do what I do if you didn't feel that way. I want you know how thankful I am."

Not only has Homer supported my going with his prayers , he has underwritten a lot of it. He has helped to finance migrant camp and Acteens Activators trips, more than he ever planned to! Martha Franks, our favorite longtime missionary to China, says Homer's crown will be one of the brightest in heaven!

So many joyful things have happened on trips I've taken to speak. The first time I spoke outside of Alabama, I went to the Oklahoma Acteens Convention in 1974. I was scared to death. When the Oklahoma Acteens and their leaders received me warmly, I was astounded. After speaking five times, I had to leave before the end of the last session to catch my flight home. I hurried down the aisle accompanied by Carolyn Hopkins who was then Oklahoma's Acteens director. Out of nowhere an Indian Acteens leader appeared before me and chanted loudly with lifted arms. I stopped and at her conclusion continued rushing down the aisle. After we had jumped into Carolyn's car and were headed to the airport, I said, "Carolyn, if that was an Indian fertility rite, Oklahoma WMU gets the baby."

Tom Thurman has said to me, "Sometimes you're hot, sometimes you're not." I apologize to all those people who have heard me speak when I've been cold—even stone cold! I have been, but I remember with joy the times that God has been in control and there has been fire. Student Week at Ridgecrest in 1986 was hot. I spoke on the final night and from the first sentence, "I know it will be hard for you to believe, but last year I went to Nigeria, Ethiopia, and Yemen," to the last phrase, "Go for it!" those students were with me. So was the Lord; the standing ovation was for what He had done!

Another sizzle that I hug to my heart were the closing meditations at WMU Weeks at Glorieta and Ridgecrest in 1976. The most difficult thing to do each night was to find a transition between what I was to say and what the preceding speaker was talking about. One night, I spoke on how I felt about being a woman. Dr. Kenneth Chafin (now at Southern Baptist Seminary in Louisville, Kentucky) was the featured speaker. He spoke of the equality, even the superiority of women. As my transition that night I said, "Lord, Dr. Chafin almost convinced me of how equal I am. Then I started to wonder why he got 45 minutes and I got 5!" That was probably the biggest laugh I ever received!

Some of the speaking has been difficult. I remember once when I was scheduled to speak in a morning worship service. I arrived to find the pastor on the front steps waiting for me. A smile was missing from his face. He looked at me disdainfully and barked, "Follow me." He led me back to his study; the deacons were assembled. He slammed the door and said, "Let us pray." Lifting his head and his voice to the heavens, he said, "Dear Lord, I've never allowed a woman behind the sacred desk. Forgive me." Imagine speaking after that!

The speaking—even the sizzling—has not been as much fun as the missions trips with the young people. I've written about some of them, but I've left out a lot. I've not written about the Acteens Activators trip to Massachusetts. We went to work with Bruce and Laura Allen who were then at First Baptist Church, Shrewsbury, Massachusetts. After sleeping on concrete floors at Taos, we stayed at Rice House and Laity Lodge, (as in early pioneer missionary Luther Rice!) We lived in luxury and history. We soaked up the history of the haystack prayer meeting and the birth of American foreign missions.

Massachusetts was our first experience in working with the up-and-outs: upper class people who were without the Lord. However, we discovered that children are children. Even though their parents were not interested, the children were. We taught 70 of them in morning and afternoon backyard Bible schools.

We loved New England and we loved those children.

I have not written about Mexico. I love Mexico and the missionaries there, especially the missionaries' kids (MKs). I was invited to go to Mexico for an MK retreat in 1986 shortly after the horrible earthquakes and the death of Mission chairman Jim Philpot. My directions were to love the MKs and to help them have a wonderful time.

I flew to Dallas/Fort Worth and boarded a flight to Guadalajara, Mexico. Immediately after we had been served lunch, the pilot reported mechanical difficulties and turned the plane back to Dallas/Fort Worth. Eight hours later, I arrived in Guadalajara, exhausted. Equally tired were the MKs and missionaries who were waiting for me to begin the long trip over the mountains to the Pacific Coast. The roads were steep, narrow, and winding, and we were forced by the late hour to travel rapidly. Can you imagine anything more mortifying than getting car sick with two van loads of teenagers watching and no place to pull over. It does not make for joy. They comforted me and told me of all their horrendous experiences on Mexico's mountains. Jackie Swan, one of my favorite Mexico missionaries, washed my horrible clothes that night unbeknownst to me. Greater love hath no friend.

The retreat turned out to be one of the most joyful weekends of my life. I hope it was the same for the absolutely greatest MKs anywhere.

Minnesota has not had a chapter. (I demand a few more chapters!) Our Acteens Activators went to Minnesota twice: in 1988 to start a church and in 1990 to begin migrant work in the state. Both experiences were fantastic.

I have not written about my love affair with North Carolina. I'd rather speak in North Carolina than anywhere else in the world. They pray better, therefore, it is easier to speak there. I've not mentioned my admiration for WMU executive director, Nancy Curtis, or former missions director for the state convention, Sara Ann Hobbs. And the prayer warriors who have prayed for me—I can't call all their names but chief among them are Betty Harris in Andrews and Dorothy Morre in Wilmington. I love North Carolina. They have sent me to places I could not go on my own, like Cherokee Indian prayer retreat in Oklahoma, one of the most joyful retreats in which I ever participated. I have wonderful friends in Tallequah, the capital of the Cherokee Indian nation.

I cannot leave out Alaska—absolutely gorgeous, absolutely freezing Alaska, even in June. We worked in GA camp at Griffin Baptist Assembly in Wasilla out from Anchorage. This was the most difficult Acteens Activators trip for me. When we left home in June 1987, my little grandson, Dane, was ill. He was almost two years old and was being tested for leukemia. I was so burdened. I'll never forget one of the most moving prayer meetings I've ever been a part of. The three Columbiana leaders, Murrel Mullins, my sister-in-law, Glenn Milstead, and I got down on the cold wooden floor of cabin 3. We were joined by Angela Jones, Mary Smith, Mary Saarloos, and Cheryl Marchuk, GA leaders from Alaska, and the four summer missionaries, Sherrie Gore, Shelly Gantt, John Siler, and Blake Westbrook all from Georgia. We lifted that precious little boy right up into the lap of the Heavenly Father. Before the week ended we knew that Dane did not have leukemia. Praise the Lord! Some months later we knew he had severe food allergies and we found the doctor who pulled him out of that threatening condition.

Not every situation has been easy or joyful. The sorrow and anxiety have taught me how to pray for miracles. I have learned that lesson well, and I have seen God bring the miracles to pass.

I have not told you about Kansas City and the beautician who fixed my hair just like Bess Truman's; I have not told you about Buffalo and sleeping in Peace Bridge Mission shortly before they tore it down. I have not told you about working with my nephew Ray Joiner in the Baptist Center in Birmingham. I haven't told you about my friend, Pro Consul General Roseargentina Pinel de Cordoba. I haven't even told you about the Sunday School class I teach—the most wonderful group of women in the world. I haven't told you about Jimmy and Charlotte Walker, our first missionary friends.

What joy! The main ingredient is joy. How can I help but praise Him and love Him and count it all joy!

YEA!!
Sometimes I get so excited
because God's side wins!
I see a teenager do something
wonderful and touching,
I see a woman put her arms
around someone hurting,
I see a man stand tall
for the right,
I see little children with shining faces
singing "Jesus loves me."

Thank you, God,
Sometimes I forget
the victory really is yours,
and I can count it all joy!